Design for Sustainability

Design for Social Responsibility Series

Series Editor: Rachel Cooper

Social responsibility, in various disguises, has been a recurring theme in design for many years. Since the 1960s several more or less commercial approaches have evolved. In the 1970s designers were encouraged to abandon 'design for profit' in favour of a more compassionate approach inspired by Papanek.

In the 1980s and 1990s profit and ethical issues were no longer considered mutually exclusive and more market-oriented concepts emerged, such as the 'green consumer' and ethical investment. The purchase of socially responsible, 'ethical' products and services has been stimulated by the dissemination of research into sustainability issues in consumer publications. Accessibility and inclusivity have also attracted a great deal of design interest and recently designers have turned to solving social and crime-related problems.

Organisations supporting and funding such projects have recently included the NHS (research into design for patient safety); the Home Office has (design against crime); Engineering and Physical Sciences Research Council (design decision-making for urban sustainability). Businesses are encouraged (and increasingly forced by legislation) to set their own socially responsible agendas that depend on design to be realised.

Design decisions all have environmental, social and ethical impacts, so there is a pressing need to provide guidelines for designers and design students within an overarching framework that takes a holistic approach to socially responsible design.

This edited series of guides is aimed at students of design, product development, architecture and marketing, and design and management professionals working in the sectors covered by each title. Each volume includes:

- The background and history of the topic, its significance in social and commercial contexts and trends in the field.
- Exemplar design case studies.
- Guidelines for the designer and advice on tools, techniques and resources available.

Design for Sustainability

A Practical Approach

TRACY BHAMRA and
VICKY LOFTHOUSE

GOWER

© Tracy Bhamra and Vicky Lofthouse, December 2007

All rights reserved. No part of this publication may be reproduced, stored in a retrieval system or transmitted in any form or by any means, electronic, mechanical, photocopying, recording or otherwise without the prior permission of the publisher.

Published by
Ashgate Publishing Limited
Wey Court East
Union Road
Farnham
Surrey, GU9 7PT
England

Ashgate Publishing Company
Suite 420
101 Cherry Street
Burlington, VT 05401-4405
USA

Tracy Bhamra and Vicky Lofthouse have asserted their moral right under the Copyright, Designs and Patents Act, 1988, to be identified as the authors of this work.

British Library Cataloguing in Publication Data
Bhamra, Tracy
　　Design for sustainability : a practical approach. – (Design
　　for social responsibility)
　　1. Design, Industrial 2. Sustainable design
　　I. Title II. Lofthouse, Vicky
　　745.2

　　ISBN–13: 9780566087042

Library of Congress Control Number: 2007931691

Reprinted 2008, 2011

Printed and bound in Great Britain by
TJI Digital, Padstow, Cornwall.

Contents

List of Figures		*ix*
List of Tables		*xi*
Acknowledgements		*xiii*
Preface		*xv*
Chapter 1	**Introduction**	**1**
	Defining Industrial Design	2
	Design for Sustainability Emerges	3
	Challenge for Design	5
Chapter 2	**Introduction to Sustainable Development**	**9**
	Sustainable Development: A Historical Perspective	9
	Understanding Sustainable Development	14
	Major Challenges to Sustainable Development	16
	Emerging Drivers for Sustainable Development	19
	Scale of Change Needed	19
	Conclusions	20
Chapter 3	**Business and Sustainable Development**	**23**
	The Business Case for Sustainable Development	23
	Business Response to Sustainable Development	24
	Legislation	30
	Conclusions	34
Chapter 4	**A New Design Focus**	**37**
	Design for Sustainability	38
	The Product Life Cycle	40
	Materials Selection	41
	Impact of Use	45
	Length of Life	50
	End of Life	51

	Needs	55
	Conclusions	58
Chapter 5	**Methods and Tools for Design for Sustainability**	**65**
	Environmental Assessment Tools	65
	Strategic Design Tools	71
	Idea Generation	78
	User Centered Design	87
	Information Provision	95
	Conclusions	99
	Further Information	99
Chapter 6	**Case Studies of Product Improvement and Redesign**	**103**
	Washing Machine, Miele GmbH	103
	Single Use Camera, Kodak Limited	105
	Ecobottle, Sarda Acque Minerali S.p.A	106
	Azur Precise Irons, Royal Philips Electronics K.V	108
	Medisure Monitored Dosing System, The Boots Company	109
	Life Chair, Formway	110
	Furniture Transport Packaging, Segis SpA	113
	Sustainable Brush Manufacturer, Charles Bentley & Sons	115
	iU22 Ultrasound Machine, Royal Philips Electronics K.V	116
	Mobile Phones, Nokia	117
	Conclusions	118
Chapter 7	**Systems and Services – Looking to the Future**	**121**
	Systems Approach to Design	121
	Services	123
	Conclusions	134
Chapter 8	**Case Studies of Systems and Services**	**139**
	Mirra Chair, Herman Miller	139
	Model U Ford	141
	EcoKitchen	143
	Carpet Tiles, InterfaceFLOR	145
	One-Time-Use Video Camcorder, Pure Digital Technologies Inc	147
	Car Clubs	149
	Digital Music Distribution	150
	Casa Quick, Allegrini S.p.A	153
	Functional Sales, AB Electrolux	154

	HiCS	156
	Conclusions	159
Chapter 9	**Doing a Sustainable Industrial Design Project**	**163**
	The Brief	163
	Concept Generation	166
	Idea Development	168
	Detail Design	169
	Moving Forward	169
Appendix		*175*
Index		*179*

List of Figures

Figure 1.1	The forces influencing Industrial Design	3
Figure 2.1	Cone of prosperity	16
Figure 4.1	The influence of designers on the development of products	38
Figure 4.2	The different elements affecting the product lifecycle	40
Figure 4.3	Compostable mobile phone case	43
Figure 4.4	Treeplast	44
Figure 4.5	'Sunrise' outdoor table	47
Figure 5.1	Design for sustainability methods and tools mapped across the product development process	66
Figure 5.2	Ecodesign Web	73
Figure 5.3	Completed Ecodesign web for Boots Isotonic drink	74
Figure 5.4	Completed Ecodesign web for a new Isotonic drink bottle concept	74
Figure 5.5	Adapted Design Abacus	75
Figure 5.6	Completed Design Abacus	76
Figure 5.7	Sample page from 'Information/Inspiration'	79
Figure 5.8	Categories covered by the Flowmaker cards	82
Figure 5.9	Creativity session	84
Figure 5.10	Participant observation exercise	88
Figure 5.11	Example of user trials in progress	89
Figure 5.12	Hidden camera observations to demonstrate how users behave whilst using mobile phones	90
Figure 5.13	Money Talks template	93
Figure 5.14	Mood boards reflecting differing visions of femininity	94
Figure 5.15	Sample page from 'Information/Inspiration'	96
Figure 5.16	Real People search page of selection categories and people	97
Figure 5.17	Sample page from Real People	98

Figure 6.1	Miele washing machine	104
Figure 6.2	Kodak single use camera	106
Figure 6.3	Close up of the Ecobottle	107
Figure 6.4	Azur Precise Iron	108
Figure 6.5	Medisure packaging	109
Figure 6.6	Formway LIFE Chair	110
Figure 6.7	Segis SpA transportation systems	114
Figure 6.8	Product range offered by Charles Bentley & Sons Ltd.	115
Figure 6.9	iU22 ultrasound system	117
Figure 6.10	Heat effects for disassembly of a Nokia mobile phone	118
Figure 7.1	Model of ecodesign innovation	123
Figure 7.2	Product-service continuum	126
Figure 7.3	Three Service Concepts	128
Figure 8.1	Mirra Chair	140
Figure 8.2	Cradle to Cradle view of the Mirra Chair	141
Figure 8.3	External and internal images of the Model U Ford	142
Figure 8.4	Data wall	144
Figure 8.5	Smart sink	145
Figure 8.6	InterfaceFLOR carpet tiles as used in the 'Evergreen Leasing' system	146
Figure 8.7	Tirex carpet tiles	147
Figure 8.8	One-Time-Use Video Camcorder, Pure Digital Technologies Inc.	148
Figure 8.9	Packaging on the One-Time-Use Video Camcorder	149
Figure 8.10	Car Clubs	150
Figure 8.11	Digital music	152
Figure 8.12	The Casa Quick Van	154
Figure 8.13	Electrolux functional sales	155
Figure 8.14	How La Fiambrera works	157
Figure 8.15	Coolboxes used in the scheme	158
Figure 9.1	Sample brief for a shower gel pack	165
Figure 9.2	Concepts for refillable shower gel packaging	167
Figure 9.3	Example sketches produced at the idea development stage	168
Figure 9.4	Example of an assembly drawing	171

List of Tables

Table 2.1	Environmental space targets for the UK	20
Table 3.1	WEEE categories and the associated recovery and reuse/recycling targets stated in the European legislation	32
Table 4.1	Differentiation of environmental design philosophies	39
Table 4.2	Summary of Maslow's Hierarchy of needs	57
Table 4.3	Max-Neef's satisfiers of human needs	59
Table 5.1	MET Matrix	68
Table 5.2	Example of a completed MET Matrix for a coffee vending machine	69
Table 5.3	Completed Eco-Indicator 99 for an electric juicer	70
Table 5.4	Feasibility assessment	85
Table 7.1	Comparison of the service and industrial economies	127
Table 7.2	Service examples	130
Table 7.3	Possible advantages and drawbacks of renting and leasing	132

Acknowledgements

This book is the result of 15 years of research, collaboration and information exchange around Design for Sustainability. During this time we have worked with many great colleagues at Loughborough University and beyond and we would like to thank them for their contributions to critical discussions and idea development over the years. We would also like to thank all the students in the Department of Design and Technology at Loughborough University with whom we have tested many of the ideas and principles outlined in this book.

In particular we would like to thank Rachel Cooper for her valuable comments during the writing of this book and the final manuscript preparations; Ricardo Victoria-Uribe for creating Figure 1.1, Figure 2.1, Figure 4.1, and Figure 4.2; Rebecca Cawtherley for creating Figure 9.4; and Debra Lilley for contributing to the section on user-focused approaches.

Finally, we would also like to thank both of our families for their patience and support.

Tracy Bhamra, PhD and Vicky Lofthouse, PhD

Preface

Concern for society has often been a theme amongst designers and craftsworkers. Indeed in the UK, Ruskin and Morris at the turn of the 20th century actively pursued design and production in the material world in a manner consistent with moral and ethical values for the benefit of the wider society. During that century the design profession grew, becoming divorced from both art and crafts and production, first with the commercial designer, then the product designer, interior designer and so on, whilst architecture continued to remain an independent profession outside the broader domains of design. During that period too, the economies of the West, consumption and the use of the world's resources continued to grow at an alarming rate, contributing to the ongoing fragility of society and planet earth.

By the 1960s designers began to actively consider the wider implications of design for society. Several approaches emerged, including green design and consumerism; responsible design and ethical consuming; ecodesign and sustainability; and feminist design. In the 1970s Papanek, amongst others, encouraged designers to abandon 'design for profit' in favour of a more compassionate approach. In the 1980s and 1990s profit and ethical issues were no longer considered mutually exclusive and more market-oriented approaches emerged, such as the 'green consumer' and ethical investment. The purchase of socially responsible, 'ethical' products and services was facilitated by the dissemination of research into sustainability in consumer publications and the emergence of retail entrepreneurs such as the late Anita Roddick of The Body Shop. Accessibility and inclusivity also saw a great deal of design interest and activity and, more recently, designers have turned to resolving issues related to crime.

At the same time governments, businesses and individuals have become increasingly aware of what we are doing, not only to the world, but also to each other. Human rights, sustainability and ethics are all issues of concern, whilst the relationship between national economies and poverty struggles to be resolved. Global businesses have recognized the changing environment and are setting their own corporate social responsibility (CSR) agendas. The World Business Council for Sustainable Development proposes that 'CSR is the continuing commitment by business to behave ethically and contribute to economic development while improving the quality of life of the workforce and their families as well as of the local community and society at large' (Moir, 2001). If businesses and organizations are to turn these ideas into reality, 'design' is an essential ingredient.

Designers make daily decisions with regard to the use of resources, and to the lifestyle and use of products, places and communications. In order to achieve the needs of businesses, the desires of the consumer and improvement of the world, the designer in making decisions must embrace dimensions of social responsibility. However, there is now a need to shift from focusing on a single issue towards taking a more holistic approach to socially responsible design. This book is part of a series that brings together the leading authors and researchers to provide texts on each of the major socially responsible dimensions. Each book in the series provides a background to the history and emergence of the topic, provides case study exemplars and indicates where the reader can access further information and help.

Tracy Bhamra and Vicky Lofthouse have been researching and teaching in the field of environmental design for fifteen years. This book is the culmination of their thinking in the field and provides an insight into how design and designers can provide for more sustainable futures. While focusing primarily on product and industrial design the theory and the tools are essential to considering sustainable design in many other design domains and as such this book provides an essential reference for designers to practice in a way that achieves a more sustainable world.

The book contributes to a series and although it can be read in isolation, the sum of designers' responsibility to society can only be entirely understood by considering all the dimensions that this series covers. However, we are only too acutely aware that the domain changes and evolves, and that the designer's major responsibility will be to continue to redefine their role in society and the influence they can make to creating a better world.

Professor Rachel Cooper
Lancaster University, UK

Introduction

CHAPTER 1

'There are professions more harmful than industrial design, but only a very few... by creating whole new species of permanent garbage to clutter up the landscape, and by choosing materials and processes that pollute the air we breath, designers have become a dangerous breed... In this age of mass production when everything must be planned and designed, design has become the most powerful tool with which man shapes his tools and environments (and, by extension, society and himself). This demands high social and moral responsibility from the designer.'

Victor Papanek (p. ix, Papanek, 1985)

Design for sustainability is part of the bigger picture of sustainable development, a subject which has received considerable media attention in recent years due to a range of world wide crises which have manifested themselves as political problems: climate change, famine, disease and poverty.

The evolution of sustainability has been described as a series of three waves, with peaks and troughs of activity, that contribute to the momentum we see today (SustainAbility, 2006). The first wave occurred in the 1960s and 1970s with the birth of the Green Movement and the rise of Non Governmental Organisations (NGOs), such as Friends of the Earth and Greenpeace, which focused on driving change via government policy and regulation.

The second wave occurred in the 1980s, set off by a range of economic crises (brought on by the collapse of the Berlin Wall) and environmental catastrophes (from Bhopal to Chernobyl) which prompted a range of legislation and environmental, healthy and safety standards. At this time NGOs used a number of high profile business transgressions to catalyse public debate and drive regulatory and market responses. The concepts of auditing, reporting and engagement within business entered the mainstream (SustainAbility, 2006).

The new millennium saw the start of the third wave of sustainability. Unrest in the Middle East and elsewhere had led to a growth in anti-globalisation, often in the guise of anti-Americanism. The first World Social Forum, organised in opposition to the World Economic Forum brought together activists and NGOs from around the world, campaigning on issues such as trade justice and debt, and increasingly united on issues of water scarcity and exploitation. In the wake of another set of high profile business fiascos such as the Enron debacle, corporate governance and liability became a hot issue for top management and for financial markets. Meanwhile, businesses started to explore new partnerships with NGOs, for example Greenpeace and Shell shared a platform at the Johannesburg Summit, also Greenpeace formed a joint venture with Innogy to create the Juice wind power brand, which recently began to feed power generated by a huge offshore wind farm into the national grid (SustainAbility, 2006).

Since the late 1960s when Victor Papanek (1971) first blamed the design profession for creating wasteful products and customer dissatisfaction, there has been a growing feeling in many environmental circles that design and manufacture is responsible for many of the man-made stresses imposed on the planet. A fact that is well illustrated by the fact 80 per cent of products are discarded after a single use and 99 per cent of materials used are discarded in the first six weeks (Shot in the Dark, 2000). Though this trend is expected to start to change with the introduction of new product focused environmental legislation, the fact still remains that mainstream product design draws on scarce resources to create and power products which often have little or no consideration for impact on society and the environment.

Defining Industrial Design

Throughout the nineteenth century, the term 'designer' was vague and ambiguous, referring to a wide range of occupations: fine artists, architects, craftsmen, engineers and inventors (Sparke, 1983). By the twentieth century the profession of design had developed into Industrial Design as we know it today, existing in design teams and governed by management structure (Sparke, 1983).

Industrial Design is a broad and complex profession (Heskett, 1991; Tovey, 1997; Industrial Design Society of America, 1999) whose evolution has been influenced by the British Arts and Crafts movement, developments in the US and the influences of the Bauhaus school of design in Germany (Heskett, 1991; Tovey, 1997). It is because of these complex roots that Industrial Design has been described as a pendulum which swings between art and engineering (Ozcan, 1999). This is a rich metaphor that creates a valuable picture of how different fields influence the subject. It can be made even more powerful, if one imagines Industrial Design to be represented by a steel plumb which is hung as a pendulum, surrounded by a series of magnetic discs, which represent the other forces which act upon it, such as the business, marketing and the consumer, as illustrated in Figure 1.1 (Lofthouse, 2001).

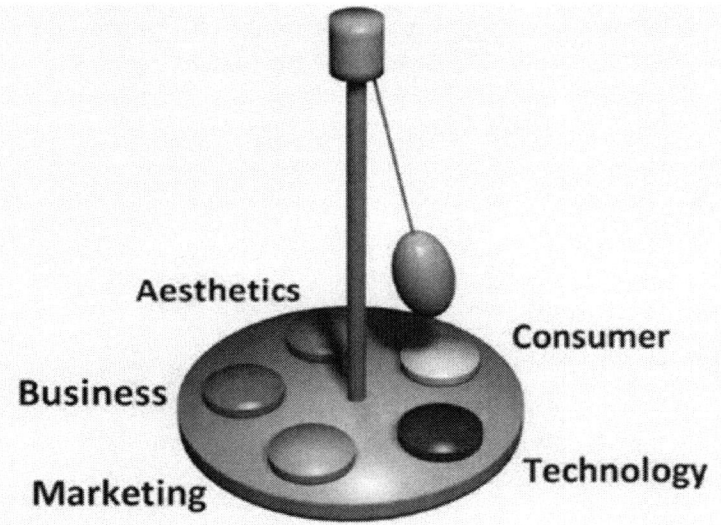

Figure 1.1 The forces influencing Industrial Design

Within industry, industrial designers tend to either work 'in-house', as a function of a larger organisation or as independent design consultants within a design consultancy that services a variety of different clients (Lofthouse, 2001). Within both of these capacities industrial designers can be involved in the design and development of both consumer and industrial goods (Lofthouse, 2001). This book focuses on consumer products. Within this sector, industrial designers can serve a wide range of industries such as pharmaceuticals, packaging, and electrical and electronic domestic products, as such their outputs can vary enormously in terms of their nature and complexity.

Design for Sustainability Emerges

The concept of design for sustainability first emerged in the 1960s when Packard (1963); Papanek (1971); Bonsiepe (1973) and Schumacher (1973) began to criticise modern and unsustainable development and suggest alternatives.

The second wave emerged in the late 1980s and early 1990s and coincided with the green consumer revolution. Writers such as Manzini (1990); Burall (1991), Mackenzie (1991) and Ryan (1993) began to call for design to make radical changes. This wave continued to gain momentum towards the end of the 1990s and early 2000s as design for sustainability became more widespread. Though there has been a long history of designers being motivated and interested in improving the environmental and social impact of the products they produce, there has been a lack of opportunity within the industrial context with case studies only starting to emerge from electronic and electrical companies in the early 1990s when companies such as Philips, Electrolux, IBM and Xerox began to promote the work they had done in this area. Although large industry commitment to integrating environmental and social issues into product development has continued to be on the rise there has been little evidence of widespread opportunity for this type of holistic thinking, in the commercial design industry.

Design for sustainability issues are currently rarely addressed in the design brief (Dewberry, 1996; Lofthouse, 2001) and as such it is often difficult for designers to have the opportunity to engage with environmentally and socially responsible design in a professional capacity. This book aims to change this situation and encourage a more widespread approach to design for sustainability.

In the past environmental and socially responsible design has not been specifically encouraged through design education and training. This is now changing – for example in the UK programmes such as STEP and Sustainable Design Awards developed and run by the charity Practical Action are set up to encourage sustainability awareness in young designers working at National Curriculum key stage 3 and 4 (ages 11–16) and A-levels respectively. Similarly projects such as DEMI, and the pioneering work of the Centre for Sustainable Design, Goldsmiths College, Loughborough University and the setting up of a Toolbox for Sustainable Design (Bhamra and Lofthouse, 2004) – which aims to help other lecturers develop sustainable design courses – have helped to change this situation.

Research in the field of design for sustainability is now well established, though it can still be considered a new area. Most of the developed nations now have some form of active research into design for sustainability, covering issues such as: implementation of legislation, eco-innovation, corporate social responsibility, product service systems, eco-redesign, impacts of user behaviour, design for disassembly and reverse manufacturing.

Challenge for Design

Part of the challenge for designers is for them to fully understand the breadth of the agenda and appreciate what can be tackled under the umbrella of design for sustainability. Within the design community there is a general lack of awareness of many issues relating to sustainable development. Designers need to understand and even communicate to their colleagues that design for sustainability is about more than recycling or using recycled materials.

Design for sustainability offers a new and broader context for designing. Birkeland (2002) encapsulates this by presenting a new vision for design which is:

- Responsible – redefining goals around needs, social/eco equity and justice.
- Synergistic – creating positive synergies; involving different elements to create systems change.
- Contextual – re-evaluating design conventions and concepts towards social transformation.
- Holistic – taking a life cycle view to ensure low impact, low cost, multi-functional outcomes.
- Empowering – fosters human potential, self-reliance and ecological understanding in appropriate ways.
- Restorative – integrates the social and natural world; recultivates a sense of wonder.
- Eco-efficient – proactively aims to increase the economy of energy, materials and costs.
- Creative – represents a new paradigm that transcends traditional boundaries of discipline thinking; to 'leapfrog'.
- Visionary – focuses on visions and outcomes and conceives of appropriate methods, tools, processes to deliver them.

Architect William McDonough and chemist Michael Braungart (2001) suggested that with hindsight the design brief for the Industrial Revolution could be rewritten. Design a system of production that:

- puts billions of pounds of toxic material into the air, water and soil;
- measures prosperity by activity, not legacy;

- requires thousands of complex regulations to keep people and natural systems from being poisoned too quickly;
- produces materials so dangerous that they will require constant vigilance from future generations;
- results in gigantic amounts of waste;
- puts valuable materials in holes all over the planet, where they can never be retrieved;
- erodes the diversity of biological species and cultural practices;

Not exactly a very positive legacy for the twentieth century!

This book aims to reverse the trend of design contributing to global environmental and social problems by inspiring and empowering you to make a difference. It hopes to enlighten you about the sustainability generally and show you how better design can improve things. By considering the environment and society when you are designing you are able to offer your clients truly *good* design that meets their requirements and those of an increasingly fragile planet. We will help you as a designer to engage with sustainability and start to make changes.

References

Bhamra, T. A. and Lofthouse, V. A. (2004), 'Toolbox for Sustainable Design Education'. Available at: www.lboro.ac.uk/research/susdesign/LTSN/Index.htm (Loughborough: Loughborough University).

Birkeland, J. (2002), *Design for Sustainability: A Sourcebook of Integrated, Eco-Logical Solutions* (Sheffield: Earthscan Publications).

Bonsiepe, G. (1973) 'Precariousness and Ambiguity: Industrial Design in Dependent Countries' in *Design for Need* Bicknell, J. and McQiston, L. (eds.) pp. 13-19 (London: Pergamon Press, The RCA).

Burall, P. (1991), *Green Design* (London: Design Council).

Dewberry, E. L. (1996), *EcoDesign – Present Attitudes and Future Directions*, Doctoral Thesis (Milton Keynes: The Design Discipline Technology Faculty Open University).

Heskett, J. (1991), *Industrial Design* (London: Thames & Hudson).

Industrial Design Society of America (1999), IDSA web site. Available at: www.idsa.org

Lofthouse, V. A. (2001), *Facilitating Ecodesign in an Industrial Design Context: An Exploratory Study*, Doctoral Thesis (Cranfield: In Enterprise Integration Cranfield University).

Mackenzie, D. (1991), *Green Design: Design for the Environment* (London: Laurence King Publishing Ltd.).

Manzini, E. (1990), 'The New Frontiers: Design Must Change and Mature', *Design*, 501, p. 9.

McDonough, W. and Braungart, M. (2001), 'The Next Industrial Revolution' in *Sustainable Solutions: Developing Products and Services for the Future* Charter, M. and Tischner, U. (eds,) pp. 139–50 (Sheffield: Greenleaf Publishing Ltd.).

Ozcan, A. C. (1999), Communication on the IDFORUM Mailbase. Accessed 8th June 1999, IDFORUM.

Packard, V. (1963), *The Waste Makers* (Middlesex: Penguin).

Papanek, V. (1971), *Design for the Real World* (New York: Pantheon Books).

Papanek, V. (1985), *Design for the Real World: Human Ecology and Social Change* (London: Thames & Hudson).

Ryan, C. (1993) 'Design and the Ends of Progress' in *O2 Event: Striking Visions*, Groen, M., Musch, P. and Zijlstra, S. (eds) (The Netherlands: O2).

Schumacher, E. F. (1973), *Small is Beautiful: a Study of Economics as if People Mattered* (London: Sphere Books, Ltd.).

Shot in the Dark (2000), *Design on the Environment: Ecodesign for Business* (Sheffield: Shot in the Dark)

Sparke, P. (1983), *Consultant Design: The History and Practice of the Designer in Industry* (London: Pembridge Press Limited).

Sustainability (2006), *Trends and Waves*. Available at: www.sustainability.com/insight/trends-and-waves.asp.

Tovey, M. (1997), 'Styling and Design: Intuition and Analysis in Industrial Design', *Design Studies*, 18, pp. 5–31. [DOI: 10.1016/S0142-694X%2896%2900006-3]

Introduction to Sustainable Development

CHAPTER

2

This chapter gives an historical overview of sustainable development. It then goes on to introduce the main principles underpinning sustainable development, summarises the key challenges and reflects on the scale of change needed to achieve it. The overarching aim is to demonstrate how and why sustainable development has become such an important issue on the world agenda.

Sustainable Development: An Historical Perspective

The term Sustainable Development was first used in 1987 in what is now known as the Brundtland Report. It was defined as '…development that meets the needs of the present without compromising the ability of future generations to meet their own needs' (World Commission on Environment and Development, 1987). However, concern about the environment and society did not start here but had been growing steadily since the 1960s and eventually led to the first Earth Summit held in Rio in 1992.

1962: Rachel Carson published her book *Silent Spring* (1962) which drew attention to the destruction of wildlife caused by the use of the insecticide DDT. Carson was a respected writer and scientist and was one of the first people to criticise this 'miracle' technology which had proven to be so effective against malaria and typhus. Unfortunately, DDT was also discovered to have a high toxicity toward fish and many species of insects developed resistance towards it. The chemical stability of DDT and its fat solubility compounded the problem as this meant DDT built up within animals over time. Carson highlighted that interfering with natural systems that we did not fully understand could have serious environmental consequences and effects on human health.

1969: Friends of the Earth was formed as a non-profit advocacy organization dedicated to protecting the planet from environmental degradation; preserving biological, cultural and ethnic diversity; and empowering citizens to have a voice in decision-making.

1970: the First Earth Day was held as a national teach-in on the environment. An estimated 20 million people participated in peaceful demonstrations across the US.

1971: Greenpeace was started up in Canada and launched an aggressive agenda to stop environmental damage through civil protests and non-violent interference. In the same year the Polluter Pays Principle was introduced by the Organisation for Economic Co-operation and Development Council (OECD), this was the first time that it was decreed that those causing pollution should pay the costs. Also the book, 'Only One Earth' was published, sounding an urgent alarm about the impact of human activity on the biosphere but raising optimism that a shared concern for the future of the planet could lead humankind to create a common future.

1972: The United Nations Conference on Human Environment was held in Stockholm under the leadership of Maurice Strong. The conference focused mainly on the regional pollution and acid rain problems of northern Europe and led to the establishment of many national environmental protection agencies and the United Nations Environment Programme (UNEP). In the same year the Club of Rome published its report Limits to Growth which was extremely controversial because it predicted dire consequences if growth was not slowed. Developed countries criticised the report for not including technological solutions while developing countries were incensed because it advocated the abandonment of economic development.

1973: The OPEC oil crisis occurred and further fuelled the limits to growth debate. This was the same year that the economist Fritz Schumacher first published his book *Small is Beautiful* (1999) which linked concern about pollution with development issues. He introduced the idea of appropriate technology as a solution for the Developing World. His ideas were controversial but were the basis for establishing the Practical Action (formerly the Intermediate Technology Development Group) who still runs projects in the Developing World using his principles.

1974: Molina and Rowland released their CFCs work in the scientific journal, *Nature* (Molina and Rowland, 1974). They calculated that the continued use of CFC gases at an unaltered rate would critically deplete the ozone layer but it wasn't until 1987 that the Montreal Protocol on Substances that Deplete the Ozone Layer was adopted.

1980: The World Conservation Strategy was released by The International Union for the Conservation of Nature and Natural Resources (now known as the World Conservation Union). The section entitles 'Towards Sustainable Development' identified the main agents of habitat destruction as poverty, population pressure, social inequity and the terms of trade. It called for a new international development strategy with the aims of redressing inequities, achieving a more dynamic and stable world economy, stimulating economic growth and countering the worst impacts of poverty. In the same year the US President Jimmy Carter authorised the study leading to the Global 2000 report. This report recognised biodiversity for the first time as a critical characteristic in the proper functioning of the planetary ecosystem.

1981: The World Health Assembly unanimously adopted a Global Strategy for Health for All by the year 2000. This affirmed that the major social goal of governments and the World Health Organisation should be the attainment of a level of health by all people of the world that would permit them to lead socially and economically productive lives.

1982: The United Nations World Charter for Nature was published. It adopted the principle that every form of life is unique and should be respected regardless of its value to humankind. It also called for an understanding of our dependence on natural resources and the need to control our exploitation of them.

1983: The United Nations General Assembly established the World Commission on Environment and Development (WCED) with the Norwegian Prime Minister Gro Harlem Brundtland as the chairperson.

1985: The World Meteorological Society, UNEP and the International Council of Scientific Unions held a meeting that reported on the build-up of CO_2 and other 'greenhouse gases' in the atmosphere. They predicted global warming would occur. In the same year British and American scientists discovered a hole in the ozone layer at the Antarctic.

1987: The World Commission on Environment and Development published *Our Common Future*, also known as the *Brundtland Report* which linked together social, economic, cultural and environmental issues and global solutions. It popularised the term 'sustainable development'. The following year the

Intergovernmental Panel on Climate Change was established to assess the most up-to-date scientific, technical and socioeconomic research in the field.

1992: The Business Council for Sustainable Development which later became the World Business Council for Sustainable Development, published *Changing Course*. This book established business interests in promoting Sustainable Development practices. In the same year the UN Conference on Environment and Development (UNCED) (also known as the Earth Summit) was held in Rio de Janeiro. Agreements were reached on Agenda 21, the Convention on Biological Diversity, and the Framework Convention on Climate Change, the Rio Declaration, and non-binding Forest Principles. In this year The Earth Council was established in Costa Rica as a focal point for facilitating follow-up and implementation of the agreements reached at the Earth Summit, and linking national Sustainable Development councils.

1993: The first meeting of the UN Commission on Sustainable Development took place with the aim of ensuring effective follow-up to UNCED, enhanced international cooperation and rationalised intergovernmental decision-making capacity.

1995: The World Summit for Social Development was held in Copenhagen. This was the first time that the international community had expressed a clear commitment to eradicate absolute poverty.

1997: The Kyoto Protocol was signed by delegates to the UN Framework Convention on Climate Change Third Conference of the Parties (COP-3). This document set goals for greenhouse gas emission reduction and established emissions trading in developed countries and the clean development mechanism for developing countries. In the same year the UN General Assembly review of Earth Summit progress gave a sober reminder that little progress had been made in implementing the Earth Summit's Agenda 21 and ended without significant new commitments.

1999: the First Global Sustainability Index was launched, tracking leading corporate sustainable development practices world wide. Called the Dow Jones Sustainability Indexes, it provided a bridge between those companies implementing sustainable development principles and investors looking for trustworthy information to guide sustainable development focused investment decisions. This was followed by the FTSE4 Good Index Series offering the same service. In May 1999 the UK's Sustainable Development

Strategy was published and defined sustainable development in terms of four objectives:

- Social progress which recognises the needs of everyone.
- Effective protection of the environment.
- Prudent use of natural resources.
- Maintenance of high & stable levels of economic growth & employment.

2000: It was recognised that almost half of the world's population now lived in cities that occupy less than 2 per cent of the Earth's land surface, but use 75 per cent of Earth's resources.

2002: The second World Summit on Sustainable Development was held in Johannesburg during which world governments, concerned citizens, UN agencies, multilateral financial institutions, and other major groups participated and assessed global change since the United Nations Conference on Environment and Development in 1992. At the Summit the following was reported:

- A third of the world's population lives in countries suffering from moderate to high water stress.
- 80 per cent of all disease in developing countries is caused by consumption of contaminated water.
- 12 per cent of bird species, 25 per cent of mammal species and 34 per cent of fish species are under threat of extinction.
- Air pollution is estimated to cause 5 per cent of the world's deaths each year.
- 113 million of the world's children do not have access to primary education while 20 per cent of adults are illiterate, two-thirds of these are women.
- Global consumption of mineral, wood, plastics and other materials increased by 240 per cent between 1960 and 1995.

The Summit's plan of implementation recognised that an unprecedented level of commitment and co-operation is required from all sectors and countries if change is going to occur. More than one hundred world leaders made a recommitment to the principles and practice of sustainable development. Leading business people from many global companies also gave their commitment to changing their practices to be more socially and environmentally responsible. This summit came to a close with a number of agreements in the key areas of: Water and sanitation, energy, global warming, natural resources and biodiversity, trade, human rights and health.

It was widely recognised that progress towards sustainable development had been much slower than required and the agreements made at this world summit were just the start of making significant changes. Action from all groups, governments, NGOs, businesses and individuals, across the world is most urgent and at the end of the summit it was hoped that the change required would pick up momentum and start to be implemented more widely.

Understanding Sustainable Development

Sustainable development is the process by which we move towards sustainability. It is underpinned by four main principles:

- Equity Today
- Environmental Justice
- Intergenerational Equity
- Stewardship

'Equity Today' is the principle of equity between different groups of people alive today. It implies that consumption and production in one community should not undermine the ecological, social, and economic basis for other communities to maintain or improve their quality of life (OECD, 2001).

'Environmental Justice' can be described as giving equal access to a clean environment and equal protection from possible environmental harm irrespective of race, income or class or any other differentiating feature of socio-economic status (OECD, 2001).

'Intergenerational Equity' is the principle of equity between people alive today and future generations. The implication is that unsustainable production and consumption by today's society will degrade the ecological, social, and economic basis for tomorrow's society, whereas sustainable development involves ensuring that future generations will have the means to achieve a quality of life equal to or better than today's (OECD, 2001).

'Stewardship' can be described as taking responsibility for the rest of life on Earth. As sustainable development recognises natural systems underpin all human systems and therefore human society cannot function without them and there are clearly limits to ways in which natural systems can be exploited (OECD, 2001).

TRIPLE BOTTOM LINE

Many describe Sustainable Development as having 'three pillars' (Elkington, 1998), economic prosperity, environmental quality and social equality. These three pillars are the components of the concept of the 'triple bottom line' (Elkington, 1998), which is used by organisations to assess their impact on society. It has also been described as 'people, profit and planet' (Elkington, 1998).

Economic bottom line

Companies are quite used to reporting a financial bottom line, which is the profit figure after deduction of costs and depreciation of capital. This is standard accounting practice. Conventional accounting pulls together, records and analyses a wide range of numerical data and this approach is often seen as a model for environmental and social accounting. However many think that even this traditional approach to reporting may need to change to reflect the new sustainable development agenda (Elkington, 1998). For example, organisations need to consider how they can be economically sustainable in the long term.

Environmental bottom line

Organisations should also consider their impact on the environment. This would include, among other things, consideration of the consumption of resources through their use of renewable and non-renewable resources, emissions to air, land and water and waste generated. As human society cannot function without the environment it can be argued that this is preconditioned and therefore the most important pillar (Nattrass and Altomore, 2001).

Social bottom line

For this the organisation must consider how it affects the social, ethical and political climate in the communities that it operates in. The social agenda for business has been around for a long time if we consider early controversies such as slavery, child labour and working conditions (Elkington, 1998). In addition many organisations are obviously concerned about their social capital and ensure that they have invested well in it. They understand that if they are respected and trusted they are more likely to be able to attract the best people to work for them and be successful as a result (Nattrass and Altomore, 2001).

Major Challenges to Sustainable Development

While sustainable development is now discussed broadly by governments, academics and companies, there are still many challenges in all economies that are preventing great moves being made. One issue in particular is the imbalance in the share of income across the world. Since 1960 the percentage of global income claimed by the richest fifth of the world's population has risen from 70.2 per cent to 82.7 per cent (Day, 1998) and the income of the poorest fifth has declined from 2.3 per cent to 1.4 per cent (see Figure 2.1). This illustrates a decline in equity today.

We can divide the world up into three different types of economies; developed, emerging and survival. Developed economies include countries such as the UK, US, Japan and Germany. India and China are examples of emerging economies, while Sudan and Sierra Leone are considered to be survival economies. Each one of these economies has different challenges to sustainability but all broadly fall into the categories of pollution, depletion and poverty (Hart, 1997).

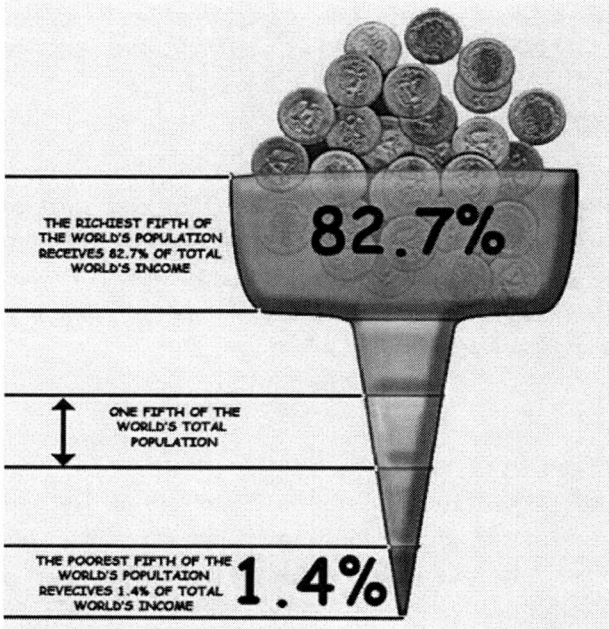

Figure 2.1   Cone of prosperity

In developed economies there are a range of challenges to sustainable development (Hart, 1997), in particular the concentrations of several greenhouse gases have increased over time due to human activities, such as the burning of fossil fuels and deforestation leading to higher carbon dioxide concentrations. The use of toxic material in manufacturing has also created many environmental problems and led to contaminated sites.

The depletion of resources within these economies is another major challenge to sustainable development. This is illustrated by the fact that total material use in Japan, Germany and the US has risen by an average of 28 per cent over the past 20 years. In addition, energy consumption in the US is projected to increase by at least 20 per cent over the next 20 years. Most of this growth will be achieved using non-renewable fossil fuels.

In general affluent societies, represented by the developed economies, account for more than 75 per cent of the world's energy and resource consumption and create the bulk of industrial, toxic and consumer waste. Developed countries have 20 per cent of the global population but are responsible for:

- 85 per cent of world consumption of aluminium and synthetic chemicals;
- 80 per cent of paper, iron and steel;
- 80 per cent of commercial energy;
- 75 per cent of timber;
- 65 per cent of meat, fertilisers and cement;
- half the world's fish and grain;
- 40 per cent of its fresh water;
- 96 per cent of radioactive waste generated;
- 90 per cent of all ozone-depleting chlorofluorocarbons (CFCs) generated.

In addition to this large consumption of resources developed economies have insufficient reuse and recycling programmes which in turn leads to more consumption. Poverty is also a problem in these economies with often high levels of unemployment in urban areas and amongst minority communities (Hart, 1997).

In emerging economies the challenges to sustainable development are quite different. For example, pollution is caused by emissions from industries which are not subject to the same level of control found within developed economies. These emissions in turn lead to the contamination of water causing problems in the environment and for humans. Another source of pollution comes from the lack of sewage treatment facilities which again leads to health problems for the population (Hart, 1997).

Depletion of resources is not just a problem in the high consuming developed economies, the emerging economies also face this particularly where there has been an overexploitation of renewable resources. In particular, across the globe more than 10% of world top soil is being eroded and consequently the available cropland is shrinking. In 1997, one-fifth of world's original forest cover remained in large tracts of undisturbed forest; however 39 per cent of what remains is threatened by ongoing or planned human activity. Linked in with this is the overuse of water irrigation for crop cultivation (Hart, 1997).

Poverty is obviously a challenge to sustainable development and one that is felt in the emerging economies by the high levels of migration to cities from rural areas. This is caused by the relative affluence of cities and the hope of employment (Hart, 1997). However, these migrants often are unable to find the employment they expect due to lack of skills. Consequently these economies offer suffer due to the lack of skilled workers in key areas such as healthcare, education, engineering and technology. This polarisation of employment opportunities between the rural and urban populations leads to increasing income inequality which is unsustainable in the long term (Hart, 1997).

There are many challenges to sustainable development within survival economies. Pollution caused by dung and wood burning in these regions directly influences the rise in greenhouse gases, the effects of which are felt around the world (Hart, 1997). The lack of sanitation in these economies is obviously one area that can lead to significant effects on the human population.

Another cause of pollution within survival economies arises from increasing development. These economies are trying to increase their development to provide a better quality of life for their populations but often by doing so ecosystems are destroyed which has knock-on effects in terms of pollution and resource depletion. As with emerging economies, survival economies also have problems with increased deforestation, soil erosion and overgrazing.

When looking at the problem of poverty in emerging economies we can see that 32 per cent of people living in these countries remain in poverty. With a continued growth in population this will not reduce in the short term. Another major challenge is that often women have a low status in society which results in them not having the same access to education and work outside the home and consequently not being involved in economic decision making. Women constitute a disproportionate share of the poor: of the estimated 1.3 billion people living in poverty, more than 70 per cent are female (Novartis Foundation for Sustainable Development, 2004).

Emerging Drivers for Sustainable Development

The RMIT Global Sustainability Institute (Karlson and Smith, 2005) has identified six types of emerging drivers for sustainable development:

1. Economic and Business Opportunities: increase productivity; create product differentiation, lean thinking; total quality management, ethically/socially responsible investment, corporate social responsibility, reduce risk of consumer boycott; NGO activities.

2. Environmental Crisis: need to restore natural capital, environmental disasters, climate change; desertification, toxic waste; insurance blowouts.

3. Staying ahead of regulation: global; national; and local.

4. Enabling technologies: ICT; ET; spatial data; renewable energy.

5. People and Populations: increasing population in developing countries, decreasing population in the Developed World, urbanisation and migration.

6. Global inequality: deep divide; access to clean water; sanitation, trade barriers; free versus fair trade, environmental refugees.

Scale of Change Needed

It is now recognised globally that change is needed if we are to progress towards a more sustainable society. One way to understand the scale of change needed is to look at what Friends of the Earth describe as Environmental Space (McLaren et al., 1997). This approach aims to help policy makers set comprehensive sustainable development targets using a framework of a range of key resources. These targets aim to help realise a more sustainable use of resources and a reduction in overall resource consumption.

The scale of these targets presents policy makers with a challenge and, whether they are set as firm policy or used to illustrate and guide policy, they demonstrate the scale of the sustainable development crisis we face and the urgency of an effective response. Some countries, in particular Denmark, Germany and the Netherlands, have begun to use the concept of Environmental Space and are consequently adopting targets. These countries have recognised that these targets can have motivational effects on businesses and the public. The adoption and logic of such targets helps governments explain what might otherwise be unpopular measures, such as new taxes (McLaren, 1997).

Table 2.1   Environmental space targets for the UK

Resource	Environmental Space person/year	Reduction required	2010 target
Aluminium	1 kg	88%	22%
Carbon dioxide (emissions)	1.1 tonnes	88%	30%
Cement	59 kg	72%	18%
Chlorine	0 kg	100%	25%
Construction aggregates	2.3 tonnes	50%	12.5%
Land (UK average quality)	0.26 hectares	27%	7%
Steel	26 kg	83%	21%
Water	187,000 l	15%	15%
Wood (Wood Raw Material Equivalent)	0.24 m3	73%	65%

Conclusions

Overall we can see that the challenge of sustainable development is one shared between Governments, NGOs, individuals and professional bodies, however, the role of business appears to be particularly significant as it is the main generator of wealth in society. To date the response from the business community has been positive and since the early 1990s many companies have reduced their environmental and social impacts to some degree. Much of this change has been voluntary rather than because of legislation and regulation. These changes though have not been enough and according to many NGOs and individual critics business is still the principal cause of much environmental damage and negative impacts on society (Nelson, 2000; Dixon, 2003). In particular there is focus on large multi-nationals that command great influence in the global economy. Many Governments, NGOs and individuals are calling for business to do much more and make a more significant move towards Sustainable Development. The following chapters will examine in more detail the business case for design for sustainability and how changes today can have significant impacts in the future.

References

Carson, R. (1962), *Silent Spring* (Boston: Houghton Mifflin).

Day, R. M. (1998), 'Beyond Eco-Efficiency: Sustainability as a Driver for Innovation', *Sustainable Enterprise Initiative*, World Resource Institute. Available at: www.wri.org/wri/meb/sei/beyond.html

Dixon, F. (2003), 'Total Corporate Responsibility: Achieving Sustainability and Real Prosperity' in *Ethical Corporation Magazine*, December 2003.

Elkington, J. (1998), *Cannibals with Forks: The Triple Bottom Line of 21st Century Business* (Oxford: Capstone Publishing Ltd.).

Hart, S. L. (1997), 'Beyond Greening: Strategies for a Sustainable World', *Harvard Business Review*, 75:1, pp. 67–76.

Karlson, C. H. and Smith, M. H. (2005), *The Natural Advantage of Nations* (London: Earthscan Publications).

McLaren, D. (1997), 'Overcoming the Barriers to Effective National Sustainable Development Strategies: The Role of Environmental Space Analysis'. Available at: www.foe.co.uk/resource/articles/overcoming_barriers_space.html

McLaren, D. P., Bullock, S. and Yousuf, N. (1997), *Tomorrow's World: Britain's Share in a Sustainable Future* (London: Earthscan Publications).

Molina, M. J. and Rowland, F. S. (1974), 'Stratospheric Sink for Chlorofluoromethanes: Chlorine Atomic-catalysed Destruction of Ozone', *Nature* 249:5460, pp. 810–12 [DOI: 10.1038/249810a0].

Nattrass, B. and Altomore, M. (2001), *The Natural Step for Business: Wealth Ecology and the Evolutionary Corporation* (Canada: New Society Publishing).

Nelson, J. (2000), 'The Leadership Challenge of Global Corporate Citizenship', *Perspectives on Business and Global Change*, 14, pp. 11–26.

Novartis Foundation for Sustainable Development (2004), 'Women in Development'. Available at: www.novartisfoundation.com/en/projects/right_health/backgrounds/ women_development.htm

Organisation for Economic Co-operation & Development – OECD (2001), *Sustainable Development: Critical Issues*. ISBN: 92-64-18695-6.

Schumacher, E. F. (1999), *Small is Beautiful: Economics as if People Mattered: 25 Years Later with Commentaries!* (Vancouver: Hartley and Marks Publishers).

World Commission on Environment and Development (1987), *Our Common Future* (New York: Oxford University Press).

Business and Sustainable Development

CHAPTER

3

This chapter examines how businesses have taken on board the challenge of sustainable development in recent years. In particular it outlines some of the different approaches that are being adopted including design for sustainability which is the focus of the whole book. Finally some of the main pieces of legislation that are driving design for sustainability are highlighted

The Business Case for Sustainable Development

The business case for sustainable development is one that first emerged in the 1970s with what the World Business Council for Sustainable Development (WBCSD) later called 'eco-efficiency': cutting costs by reducing the resource intensity of a company's operations. Since then things have changed quite significantly and in 2002 Forum for the Future published their report 'Sustainability Pays' drawing on the findings of almost 400 research papers outlining the business case for sustainable development. This report identified four main areas where sustainable development policies have brought companies financial benefits (Forum for the Future, 2002).

Firstly it outlined how leading companies can benefit and gain an advantage from being the first-mover. In addition, organisations can demonstrate enlightened and effective management by addressing social and environmental issues; this in turn can attract investment and motivate employees. The corporate reputation can benefit significantly if the company is seen to act responsibly, adding to the intangible assets of the firm. Finally, engaging with sustainable development requires innovation across the company which stimulates new market opportunities.

It was during the 1970s when companies first began to be proactive about environmental issues and identify ways in which they could change their practices to consider the environment and, more recently, the social aspects of their operations. Much of the early work by companies focused on the 'clean up' of waste and pollution to avoid hefty fines. However, as time progressed companies began to realise that this was not the most cost-effective way to deal with environmental problems and so their focus shifted to implementing 'end-of-pipe' technology to prevent pollution leaving their processes. Again, the realisation grew that the situation could be further improved not only from an environmental perspective but also a financial one by redesigning processes to prevent pollution or waste arising in the first place. This approach became known as cleaner production.

Since the 1980s there has been a great deal of government funding in the UK for schemes which can be described as 'Good Housekeeping' whereby resources are saved by looking at any areas of waste in the process or business. Much of this work has focused on saving money through evaluation of raw materials used in production, the waste arising at the end of production and the use of energy throughout the business. As any savings made in these areas translate directly into financial savings for the business this has been a very popular way forward.

Since the late 1990s many companies have moved on from cleaner production processes to begin to consider how to produce more sustainable products. To a certain extent this has been led by legislation but in other cases it has been part of improving the company's image with regard to sustainability that has resulted in this refocusing of design.

Business Response to Sustainable Development

Organisations need to be able to understand how they can contribute to sustainable development and the benefit of considering this as part of their business. This can prove to be a challenge for many organisations and one that needs to be considered at a strategic level. Consequently, approaches and tools have been developed to help organisations understand the principles of sustainable development and apply them to their business. This section will discuss some of the most popular of these approaches.

CORPORATE SOCIAL RESPONSIBILITY

Corporate social responsibility (CSR) is an expression used to describe a company's obligation to consider the needs of all of its stakeholders. Stakeholders are those who are influenced by, or can influence, a company's decisions and actions. These can include employees, customers, suppliers, community organisations, local neighbourhoods, investors, and shareholders.

CSR is closely linked with the principles of sustainable development in proposing that companies should be obliged to make decisions based not only on the economic factors but also on the social and environmental consequences of their activities. Some investors have begun to take account of a company's CSR policy in making investment decisions (known as ethical investing). Some consumers are also starting to become aware of the CSR performance of companies from which they buy products and services. These trends have contributed to the pressure on companies to operate in an economically, socially and environmentally sustainable way.

It is important to distinguish CSR from philanthropy, as companies have often, in the past, spent money on community projects and encouraged their employees to volunteer to take part in community work. CSR goes beyond charity and requires that a responsible company take into full account their impact on all stakeholders and on the environment when making decisions. This requires them to balance the needs of all stakeholders with their need to make a profit and reward their shareholders adequately.

A widely quoted definition by the World Business Council for Sustainable Development (1999) states that 'Corporate social responsibility is the continuing commitment by business to behave ethically and contribute to economic development while improving the quality of life of the workforce and their families as well as of the local community and society at large'.

FIVE CAPITALS

The Five Capitals approach is a strategic tool developed by Forum for the Future in the UK to aid organisations embarking on change around sustainable development principles. The Five Capitals model enables companies to build the business case for sustainable development by examining five types of sustainable capital which the economy and every organisation needs in order to function properly. The model is used to show stocks and flows of resources as they relate to a sustainable society and economy and groups together (Wilsdon, 1999, Forum for the Future, 2006):

- Natural capital – is any stock or flow of energy and matter that results in valuable goods and services. It falls into several categories: *resources*, some of which are renewable (timber, grain, fish and water), and others that are not (fossil fuels); *sinks* which absorb, neutralise or recycle wastes; and *processes*, such as climate regulation.

- Human capital – consists of health, knowledge, skills and motivation, all of which are required for productive work. Enhancing human capital (for instance, through investment in education and training) is central to a flourishing economy.

- Social capital – is the value added to any activity or economic process by human relationships and co-operation. Social capital takes the form of structures or institutions which enable individuals to maintain and develop their human capital in partnership with others, and includes families, communities, businesses, trade unions, schools, and voluntary organisations.

- Manufactured capital – is made up of material goods – tools, machines, buildings, and other forms of infrastructure – which contribute to the production process, but do not become part of its output.

- Financial capital – plays an important role in the economy, by reflecting the productive power of the other types of capital, and enabling them to be owned and traded. However, unlike the other types, it has no intrinsic value, its value is purely representative of natural, human, social or manufactured capital.

NATURAL STEP

The Natural Step Framework is a way of describing sustainability and measuring progress towards it. It was established in Sweden by Dr Karl Henrik Robert in 1989. Its purpose is to teach and support sustainability systems thinking in a range of different types of organisations through an easily understood process rooted in fundamental science. The application of the science-based framework is the way in which organisations can begin to understand what sustainability means to them. It provides a straightforward way of identifying and analysing problems. The Natural Step Framework is based on a set of scientific system conditions that define basic conditions for sustainability, providing a decision making process for organisations that are trying to become more sustainable (Nattrass and Altomore, 2001).

The system conditions are that in a sustainable society, nature is not subject to systematically increasing:

- Concentrations of substances extracted from the earth's crust;
- Concentrations of substances produced by society;

- Degradation by physical means and;
- In society human needs are met worldwide.

Companies who have worked with The Natural Step have found that their approach not only benefits the environment and society but also delivers business benefits.

> **McDonald's and The Natural Step**
>
> Since as far back as 1993 McDonald's Sweden have been talking to the Natural Step about helping to take the company in a more sustainable direction. The Natural Step helped the company examine its biggest impact and subsequently launched a number of different sustainability initiatives. Today McDonald's Sweden runs 75 per cent of their 233 stores on renewable energy, serves organic ice cream, cake and milk and recycles 90 per cent of its restaurant waste. It has also reduced the heavy metals used in construction and toys and eliminated over 1200 tonnes of packaging materials, cut waste by 85 per cent and boosted the morale of its employees – this has led to better service and happier customers.
>
> Back in the US executives at McDonald's headquarters started to take notice and asked The Natural Step to start to train their senior mangers and give them sustainability tools that would help them act as change agents throughout the company. A sustainability analysis of their whole business was also conducted and subsequently McDonald's have started to build a vision of a sustainable global food supply chain. This has meant educating their suppliers and beginning to create more sustainable solutions and setting new industry standards (The Natural Step, 2003).

ECO-EFFICIENCY

Eco-efficiency is a philosophy that encourages business to search for environmental improvements which also yield economic benefits. It focuses on business opportunities and allows companies to become more environmentally responsible and more profitable. It is often described as creating more value with less impact or doing more with less.

Eco-efficiency opportunities can emerge at any point in the entire life cycle of a product. Improving eco-efficiency does not, however, lead automatically to sustainability. Simply improving in relative terms (value per impact) may still mean an overall increase in an activity's impact and create unacceptable harm or irreversible damage. Others call for eco-effectiveness rather than efficiency, stressing the importance of innovation. Critics maintain that incremental improvements in efficiency distract attention from the innovation needed to achieve real improvements and changes in behaviour. Arguing that the environmental footprint of the rich is too big, they demand *sufficiency* instead of efficiency.

The business rationale for eco-efficiency is straightforward: it makes good business sense and being efficient is usually a priority for every company. The business case for eco-efficiency applies to every area of activity within a company – from eliminating risks and finding additional savings through to identifying opportunities and realising them in the marketplace. Eco-efficiency calls for businesses to achieve more value from lower inputs of materials and energy and with reduced emissions. It applies throughout a company, to marketing and product development as much as to manufacturing or distribution (World Business Council for Sustainable Development, 2000).

There are three broad objectives of eco-efficiency:

1. **Reducing the consumption of resources**: This includes minimising energy, materials, water and land use, enhancing recyclability and product durability, and closing material loops.

2. **Reducing the impact on nature**: This includes minimising air emissions, water discharges, waste disposal and the dispersion of toxic substances, as well as using renewable resources sustainably.

3. **Increasing product or service value**: This means providing more benefits to customers through product functionality, flexibility and modularity, providing additional services (such as maintenance, upgrading and exchange services) and focusing on selling the functional needs that customers actually want. Selling a service instead of the product itself raises the possibility of the customer receiving the same functional need with fewer materials and less resources. It also improves the prospects of closing material loops because responsibility and ownership, and therefore concern for efficient use, remain with the service provider (World Business Council for Sustainable Development, 2000).

DESIGN FOR SUSTAINABILITY

Design for sustainability can offer organisations the opportunity to enhance their sustainability performance, while simultaneously improving their profitability. Companies that apply design for sustainability find that it:

- Reduces the environmental impact of their products/processes.
- Optimises raw material consumption and energy use.
- Improves waste management/pollution prevention systems.
- Encourages good design and drives innovation.

- Cuts costs.
- Meets user needs and wants by exceeding current expectations for price, performance and quality.
- Increases product marketability.
- Improves the organisation's image.

Design for sustainability can also provide a means for establishing a long-term strategic vision of a company's future products and operations. In general, sustainable design is an enabling force to shape more sustainable patterns of production and consumption. It also provides the opportunity for organisations to increase innovation, it can offer a greater ability to compete, add value and attract customers, and enable them to become more cost-effective by reducing environmental impacts and potential liability.

By incorporating design for sustainability into product design and development, organisations gain a fresh perspective on established practices, resulting in new ideas and solutions. For example, this can result in:

- New product and/or service concepts.
- Alternative production techniques.
- Increased employee participation and satisfaction.
- Greater employee creativity.

There is also a growing global demand for sustainability features in products and services. Incorporating issues of design for sustainability into product design can help companies to meet these emerging market demands, differentiate their products in the marketplace, improve their image, win new customers and attract investment.

Design for sustainability often identifies opportunities for cost-reduction across many stages of a product's life and ensures the greatest reductions are achieved. The results are often reduced production costs, increased product quality, and increased return on environmental investments.

By decreasing a product's impact on the environment design for sustainability helps companies to ensure compliance with environmental regulations, reduce uncertainty with respect to future environmental requirements, achieve better community relations and contribute to a better local, regional and global environment.

Finally, there is also the opportunity with design for sustainability for an organisation to gain a systems view of their business. Design which focuses on a product's life cycle, helps companies create clear links between product design, supply chain management and sales/marketing, providing a mechanism for multidisciplinary teams to continuously improve products. The benefits of taking a systems view will be discussed in more detail in Chapter 7

Legislation

Legislation is a key driver for design for sustainability. A number of key pieces instigated by the EU are introduced below.

In the European Union Extended Producer Responsibility Legislation currently applies to Vehicles, Electronic and Electrical Products, Packaging and Batteries and is likely to be extended to cover further product categories in the future. Japan has similar legislation called the Home Appliance Recycling Law (Harl) which came into force in April 2001 and provides for 3 R (reduce, reuse, recycle) measures to be taken by business in the production stage. This includes design, labelling for separate collection and the development of an end-of-life take back system.

In the US many individual states have started to introduce legislation that deals with waste electronics, some examples include:

- Arkansas Computer and Electronic Solid Waste Management Act – Requires state agencies to develop and implement plans to manage and sell surplus computer equipment and electronics.

- California Electronic Waste Recycling Act – imposes an advanced recovery fee on the sale of electronic products.

- California Cell Phone Recycling Act – makes it illegal for a retailer to sell a cell phone if they do not have a collection, reuse and recycling program in place.

- Virginia Cathode Ray Tube Recycling Program – encourages cathode-ray tube and electronics recycling.

Much more state legislation is now being developed across the whole of the US and is likely to come into force in the near future. However at a federal level the Environmental Protection Agency (EPA) prefers not to legislate but instead initiate programmes to encourage waste recycling and promote improvements in design and manufacture (EPA, 2006).

END OF LIFE VEHICLE DIRECTIVE

From 1st January 2006 vehicles in the UK reaching the end of their life have had to undergo some recovery. This legislation covers all end of life vehicles (ELVs) with or without their original components fitted. There are some exemptions which apply in the case of special purpose vehicles (ambulances, fire engines, and so on). The ELV Directive comes from the European Union and all member states are obliged to implement this legislation which aims to ensure all ELVs are treated by authorised dismantlers to new environmental treatment standards. Overall the legislation seeks to increase the reuse and recovery of ELVs to a minimum of 85 per cent per vehicle by 2006, with reuse and recycling at 80 per cent. These targets are likely to increase to 95 per cent and 85 per cent by 2015 (Department of Trade and Industry, 2004a) Another key aim is to ensure that vehicle producers design vehicles with recycling in mind and restrict or ban the use of hazardous substances.

Sicne January 2007 producers have been obliged to meet all (or a significant part) of the costs of implementation, this includes the take back of the end of life vehicles from consumers and the cost of recovery.

WASTE ELECTRICAL & ELECTRONIC EQUIPMENT DIRECTIVE

Introduced into UK law in 2005, the Waste Electrical and Electronic Equipment (WEEE) Directive requires all producers of electrical and electronic equipment to take financial responsibility for what happens to the products they produce, once they reach the end of their lives. A key aim is to reduce the amount of electronic waste (e-waste) going to landfill (in 2004 this was 1 million tonnes *per annum*; Holdway and Walker, 2004). Any companies who do not comply will not be able to sell their products in European countries. The only exclusion is for very small businesses that have a turnover of less than €2 million and less than 10 employees. Producers must arrange and meet the cost of the dismantling, recovery, reuse and recycling of WEEE. This must all be done in an environmentally sound way.

The WEEE Directive specifically sets reuse/recycling and recovery targets for ten different categories of e-waste. Table 3.1 outlines the categories and their associated targets.

This legislation became operational in July 2007 in the UK, other European countries such as Denmark, the Netherlands and Germany are further along with this legislation than the UK and producers have been obliged to take back their products for a number of years.

Table 3.1   WEEE categories and the associated recovery and reuse/recycling targets stated in the European legislation (European Parliament and the Council of the European Union, 2003)

	Recovery target	Reuse/ Recycling target
Category 1. Large Household appliances (for example refrigerators, freezers, washing machines, clothes dryers, dishwashing machines, cooking, electric stoves, electric hot plates, microwaves, electric heating appliances, electric fans, air conditioner appliances)	80%	75%
Category 2. Small Household appliances (for example vacuum cleaners, carpet sweepers, appliances for sewing, knitting, weaving, irons, toasters, fryers, grinders, coffee machines, equipment for opening or sealing containers, electric knives, appliances for hair-cutting, hair-drying, tooth-brushing, shaving, massage, clocks, watches, scales.)	70%	50%
Category 3. IT and telecommunications equipment (for example mainframes, minicomputers, printer units, personal computing, personal computers, laptop computers, printers, copying equipment, electrical and electronic typewriters, pockets and desk calculators, faxes, telephones, answering systems)	75%	65%
Category 4. Consumer equipment (for example radio sets, television sets, video cameras, video recorders, hi-fi recorders, audio amplifiers, musical instruments)	75%	65%
Category 5. Lighting equipment (for example luminaires for fluorescent lamps with the exception of luminaires in households, straight fluorescent lamps, compact fluorescent lamps, high intensity discharge lamps, including pressure sodium lamps and metal halide lamps, low pressure sodium lamps)	70%	50%
Category 6. Electrical and electronic tools (with the exception of large-scale stationary industrial tools) (for example drills, saws, sewing machines, equipment for turning, milling, sanding, grinding, riveting, nailing or screwing or removing rivets, nails or screws, welding, soldering, spraying, spreading, mowing)	70%	50%
Category 7. Toys, leisure and sports equipment (for example electric trains or car racing sets, hand-held video game consoles, video games, computers for biking, and so on, sports equipment with electric or electronic components, coin slot machines.)	70%	50%
Category 8. Medical devices (with the exception of all implanted and infected products) (for example radiotherapy equipment, cardiology, dialysis, pulmonary ventilators, nuclear medicine, laboratory equipment for in vitro diagnosis, analysers, freezers, fertilisation tests)	70%	50%
Category 9. Monitoring and control instruments (for example smoke detector, heating regulators, thermostats, measuring, weighing or adjusting appliances for household or as laboratory equipment)	70%	50%
Category 10. Automatic dispensers (for example automatic dispensers for hot drinks, bottles or cans, solid products, money)	80%	75%

An accompanying piece of legislation is the Restriction of Hazardous Substances (RoHS) Directive which bans and restricts certain hazardous substances from products (see Appendix).

PACKAGING & PACKAGING WASTE DIRECTIVE

The EU Packaging & Packaging Waste Directive is concerned with the minimisation of waste and the amount of packaging material that should be recycled. It promotes and sets targets for energy recovery, re-use and recycling of packaging.

The directive sets out packaging waste targets of 60 per cent overall recovery and 55–80 per cent recycling of packaging waste (Department of Trade and Industry, 2005). This directive is unique in that it specifically links to design by setting out the 'Essential Requirements' of packaging that must be met before packaging can be placed on the UK market. These requirements outline issues which should be considered in the design and manufacture of packaging. In particular packaging volume and weight must be the minimum amount to maintain necessary levels of safety, hygiene and acceptance for the packed product and for the consumer. Packaging must be recoverable in accordance with specific requirements. Noxious or hazardous substances in packaging must be minimised in any emissions, ash or leachate, from incineration or landfill (Department of Trade and Industry, 2005).

The UK is one of the few countries (along with France and the Czech Republic) to actively enforce the Essential Requirements in the law. In the UK the government has produced comprehensive guidance notes to help companies implement these requirements in design (Department of Trade and Industry, 2004b).

BATTERIES DIRECTIVE

The Batteries Directive is a proposed piece of European Legislation. The draft Directive aims to maximise the separate collection and recycling of spent batteries and accumulators, and to reduce the disposal of batteries and accumulators in the municipal waste stream. One of the key requirements of the legislation is a partial ban on portable nickel-cadmium batteries (excludes batteries used in medical equipment, emergency lighting and alarm systems). In addition the legislation sets collection targets for spent portable batteries of 25 per cent of average annual sales 4 years after the directive is implemented in the UK, rising to 45 per cent after 8 years. It also bans the disposal of untreated automotive and industrial batteries in landfill or by incineration (Council of the European Union, 2005a).

ENERGY USING PRODUCT DIRECTIVE

The European Union is currently developing a framework for the Energy using Product (EuP) Directive which aims to set energy efficiency and other ecodesign requirements for energy-using products. This will be applied to any product that uses energy to perform its task, but is likely to only cover those that use electricity, solid, liquid and gaseous fuels. One of the key differences between this proposed legislation and the WEEE Directive is that component part manufacturers, and not just the whole product manufacturers, will be affected. The directive will encourage manufacturers to look closely at the entire life cycle of their product and make an environmental assessment (Council of the European Union, 2005b; Department of Trade and Industry, 2005) to consider:

1. Raw materials used.
2. Acquisition.
3. Manufacturing.
4. Packaging, transport and distribution.
5. Installation and maintenance.
6. Use.
7. End of Life.

The assessment will include the consumption of materials and energy, emissions to the environment, expected waste and ways of recycling and reuse. Following this assessment, design would need to ensure that it has considered the findings to try to minimise overall environmental impact of the product or component.

Overall the European Union is hoping to ensure that products that fulfil the requirements of the legislation will benefit both businesses and consumers, by facilitating free movement of goods and by enhancing product quality and environmental protection.

Conclusions

Since the 1970s the level of thinking regarding sustainable development and the nature of approaches applied by business has matured considerably. In general businesses are now taking a much more proactive and positive view of sustainable development. Corporate social responsibility and sustainability reporting is now widespread across all industrial sectors and many companies are keen to emphasise their work in this area. The stock market has also begun to take note with the FTSE 4 Good Index in the UK and the Dow Jones Sustainability Index in the US having an influential role within the markets.

As this chapter has outlined those businesses who design and manufacture product have responsibilities towards sustainable development and can use design for sustainability to make significant improvements.

References

Council of the European Union (2005a), 'Directive of the European Parliament and of the Council on Batteries and Accumulators and Waste Batteries and Accumulators and Repealing Directive 91/157/EEC'. Available at: www.dti.gov.uk/sustainability/ep/Latest_Council_draft_March05.pdf

Council of the European Union (2005b), 'Establishing a Framework for the Setting of Ecodesign Requirements for Energy-Using Products'. Available at: www.dti.gov.uk/sustainability/EuP_OJ_Text_July2005.pdf

Department of Trade and Industry (2004a), 'End of Life Vehicles (ELV)'. Available at: www.dti.gov.uk/sustainability/ELV.htm

Department of Trade and Industry (2004b), 'Packaging (Essential Requirements) Regulations Government Guidance Notes'. Available at: www.dti.gov.uk/sustainability/Essential_Req_Guidance_Notes.pdf

Department of Trade and Industry (2005), 'EC Packaging and Packaging Waste Directive 94/62/EC'. Available at: www.dti.gov.uk/sustainability/packaging.htm

EPA (2006), 'Activities Promoting EPA's Goals for Electronics'. Available at: www.epa.gov/epr/products/ele-programs.htm

European Parliament and the Council of the European Union (2003), 'Directive 2002/96/EC of the European Parliament and of the Council of 27 January 2003 on Waste Electrical and Electronic Equipment (WEEE)' in *Official Journal of the European Union*, pp. 1–15.

Forum for the Future (2002), 'Changing Business: How Forum for the Future Engages with the Business Community' *Forum for the Future*, 28, p. 28.

Forum for the Future (2006), 'Visioning and Strategy'. Available at: www.forumforthefuture.org.uk/business/businessvisioning_page94.aspx

Holdway, R. and Walker, D. (2004), 'The End of Life as We Know It' *Engineering Designer*, Mar/Apr, pp. 7–8 (Faversham: Deeson Group Ltd).

Nattrass, B. and Altomore, M. (2001), *The Natural Step for Business: Wealth Ecology and the Evolutionary Corporation* (Canada: New Society Publishing).

The Natural Step (2003), 'McDonalds Corporation Case Summary'. Available at: www.naturalstep.org.nz/downloads/International_Case_Study_pdfs/TNSI_McDonalds_corp[1].pdf

Wilsdon, J. (1999), *The Capitals Model: A Framework for Sustainability* (London: Forum for the Future).

World Business Council for Sustainable Development (1999), *CSR: Meeting Changing Expectations,* pp. 1–36 (Geneva: World Business Council for Sustainable Development).

World Business Council for Sustainable Development (2000), *Eco-efficiency Creating More Value with Less Impact* (Geneva: World Business Council for Sustainable Development).

A New Design Focus   CHAPTER 4

The design stages of the product development process have a direct influence over about 70 per cent (Fabrycky, 1987) of the final product as this is where the most critical decisions with respect to: cost, appearance, materials selection, innovation, performance, environmental impact, and perceptions of quality such as longevity, durability, reparability are made. As such, designers have an unprecedented opportunity to influence the impact that products have on the environment and society (see Figure 4.1 overleaf).

With opportunity, however, comes responsibility. As designers we have a staggering sphere of influence – and each of the choices we make filters through to the people and places affected by this influence. A newspaper report on the creation of the Dell Inspiron 600m notebook (laptop computer) clearly illustrated just how far the decisions designers make can reverberate, as it describes an enormous supply chain of about 400 companies from North America, Europe, and Asia who were involved in the development of the product (Friedman, 2005).

Our decisions have positive and negative social and environmental impacts which ricochet around the world. For example, the nature and substance of the materials that we specify will impact the communities who provide the labour to mine, process, and deliver these materials, and the land from which they are taken. These decisions can lead to positive social impacts such as the provision of reliable labour and fair income streams which lead to improved healthcare and education, or negative social impacts such as unfair pay, child labour, slavery and civil war (Cellular news, ND).

Designers have to take further responsibility because of the role they play as industry's connection with the marketplace, interacting between people and products. Designers can directly influence the decisions people make about *what they buy* and *why*. These decisions reflect peoples' perceptions of lifestyle and their associated status in the world. Lifestyle is about identity choices,

Figure 4.1 The influence of designers on the development of products

about how individuals wish to be and how they wish to be seen by others. Often this is expressed through what they consume from the material, aesthetic and symbolic perspective. Lifestyles are patterns of actions that differentiate between people. They map onto conventional social categories of class, income, age, gender and ethnicity and also transcend them. Design for sustainability can help people question what it is they are trying to gain through the purchasing decisions that they make. With the right training industrial designers have the opportunity to influence attitudes and aspirations in order to reduce users' consumption levels (Sherwin and Bhamra, 1998).

The decisions that designers make also have the opportunity to influence the way that consumers behave. For example, if a designer decides to include a stand by option on the portable television she is designing, she is providing future users with the opportunity to behave in a wasteful manner. Research has shown that stand by facilities use 8 per cent of all domestic electricity (Smith and Henderson, 2006). Whereas the decision to leave out that function would by default encourage more sustainable behaviour. The section on 'impact of use' later in the chapter demonstrates different ways that designers can encourage sustainable behaviour.

Design for Sustainability

Chapter 3 illustrated that there are many business benefits to adopting design for sustainability principles and that to be most effective these decisions need to be integrated at a strategic level. For companies that are involved in product manufacture this means that their designers need to better understand the negative environmental and social impacts of the products they produce and understand how to make the required changes to develop products which contribute to a sustainable business. The ultimate aim for businesses should be to design and develop profitable products which are both environmentally and socially responsible.

ECODESIGN AND DESIGN FOR SUSTAINABILITY

Over the years environmental philosophies have evolved from green design to ecodesign through to design for sustainability (see Table 4.1)

Good design will ensure a product contains a rationalised number of materials and components; that consumer health and safety issues are considered; that it functions appropriately and effectively and communicates this function clearly; that it is 'styled' appropriately; is ergonomically correct and complies with legislation requirements. Ecodesign goes further by aiming to reduce the environmental impact of each stage of the product life cycle.

As illustrated in Figure 4.2, in product development terms, the product life cycle covers the whole life of the product from 'cradle to grave', including: the extraction of the raw materials to make the product, the manufacturing process; its distribution, its use and what happens to it at the end of its life. Ecodesign is concerned with improving the environmental impact at each of these stages.

Design for sustainability goes further still to include the consideration of social issues such as usability, socially responsible use, sourcing and designing to address human needs. However many of these issues are often considered under a range of other banners such as ergonomics, inclusive design, design for the aged, and design against crime rather than under the overall remit of

Table 4.1 Differentiation of environmental design philosophies

Green Design	Green design focuses on single issues, for example the inclusion of recycled or recyclable plastic, or consideration of energy consumption.
Ecodesign	Environmental considerations are considered at each stage of the design process.
Design for sustainability	Design that considers the environmental (for example resource use, end of life impact) and social impact of a product (for example usability, responsible use).
Sustainability	Sustainability is considered to be more of a direction than a destination that we will actually reach.

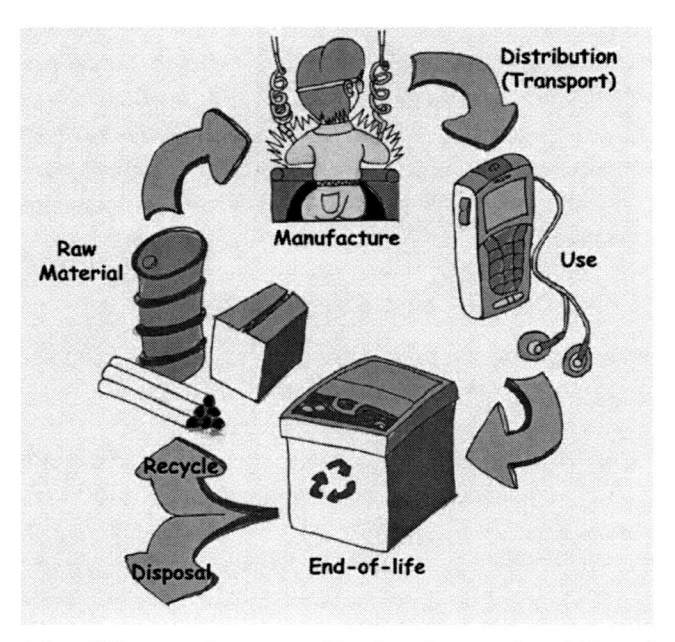

Figure 4.2 The different elements affecting the product lifecycle

design for sustainability, which will not be covered in this book. Furthermore, some social issues such as sustainable procurement, ethical finance, and ethical labour sourcing fall outside the remit of the designer as they need dealing with at a strategic level. Alternatively, design for sustainability can be approached in a completely different way by focusing on needs.

This chapter will consider the ways in which designers can reduce the environmental and social impact across the life cycle and then reflect on how a needs-focused approach to design can also be taken.

The Product Life Cycle

'Designers can make a significant difference to the effect of a product because they are responsible for influencing the key decisions. These determine the choice of materials; how long the product will last; how effectively it uses energy, and how easily it may be reclaimed and re-used.' (p. 68) (Mackenzie, 1991)

Environmental impacts occur at every stage of the product life cycle, but where the greatest impact occurs depends on the nature of the product. The greatest environmental impact of teak garden furniture is likely to be during the extraction of the raw materials, whereas for household appliances the greatest environmental impact comes from the energy consumed during the use phase (Environmental Change Unit, 1997).

When engaged in ecodesign the designer's role is to minimise these impacts by considering the environmental impacts of each stage, during the development process. There are certain key areas that designers can influence when it comes to the design of a product and its packaging. Specifically these are: materials choice, the way the product is used, length of life, type and efficiency of energy usage, how the product will be dealt with at the end of its life, how to deliver the function and whether the product is needed in the first place. The specifics associated with decisions relating to these areas will be discussed in more detail in the following sections.

Materials Selection

At a student level designers have a lot of influence over the materials which are selected in product development. As such there is an early belief that materials specification decisions can have a considerable influence on the environmental performance of the products they create. Though this is true to a certain extent, the degree of flexibility in material selection depends on the nature of the products being designed and the industry they are being designed for. Designers of medical or pharmaceutical devices, for example, are often limited to using specific grades within a given polymer type due to the regulatory requirements of the industry. Similarly designers who focus on the redevelopment of core products for large manufacturers such as Electrolux, are limited on the types of materials they can specify. For example, in the 1990s Electrolux policy specifically stated that steel should be used in the manufacture of cookers. Materials selection is not the only issue that designers' need to be aware of, as such they also have a responsibility to consider bigger questions, whether the product is actually needed and how this need can best be delivered. These issues are discussed in more detail later in the chapter.

A common question that designers ask environmental scientists is 'which material is best'? Unfortunately, there is generally no easy answer to this question as each individual product will have different requirements which will effect materials selection, such as function, planned life expectancy and required aesthetics, which will lead to different options for making an environmental choice. The key for the designer is to try and understand what characteristics the material needs to have and then match the material accordingly, while being aware that some materials have more favourable characteristics than others.

MAINSTREAM MATERIALS

Most mainstream products are made from plastics such as polypropylene (PP), polyethylene (PE), Polyethylene Terephthalate (PET), Acrylonitrile butadiene styrene (ABS), polystyrene (PS), glass or metals such as aluminium and steel. Although none of these materials are renewable, steel, aluminium, PE, PET, ABS and glass can be easily and economically recycled. They also have excellent structural and manufacturing qualities not afforded many other alternatives. The general rule of thumb for plastics, is to keep it simple. On the one hand, the more pigments, plasticisers, fire retardants and other additives are used, the worse the environmental performance becomes, however, on the other hand physical attributes such as flexibility, fire safety and UV resistance can be vital to performance. In other words compromises must be made (Datschefski, 2004). As ceramics generally have much lower embodied energy than plastics or metals, they can provide a more sustainable materials option for the right applications, such as knives and engine parts (Datschefski, 2004).

BIODEGRADABLE MATERIALS

Biodegradable materials can be broken down to their constituent parts by naturally occurring chemical compounds at the end of their useful life. Though they may be natural or synthetic in origin, natural materials such as bioplastics made from a plant-based material such as starch or polylactic acid, are greatly favoured over petrochemical variants which waste natural resources that could otherwise be recycled.

Biodegradable materials are currently used in the manufacture of bags, cutlery, pens, clothing, credit cards, food packaging, agricultural films, teabags, coffee filters, diapers and napkins (Datschefski, 2004). However, one of the key issues to recognise is that to actually degrade, materials often have to pass through a specific set of environmental conditions. Unless consumers are told that they need to put their packaging, cutlery or credit cards on the compost heap, and are encouraged to act accordingly, the product will not biodegrade and the functionality of the material will be wasted.

Engineers at Warwick University worked with hi tech materials company PVAXX Research and Development Ltd and Motorola to create a mobile telephone case that could be placed in compost in such a way that within weeks the case would begin to disintegrate releasing a seed which would grow and turn into a flower (University of Warwick, 2004). (See Figure 4.3).

Figure 4.3 Compostable mobile phone case
Reproduced with permission of © University of Warwick

RENEWABLE MATERIALS

Renewable materials such as wood, wool, paper, hemp, leather, sisal, jute, cotton and bioplastics are harvested from sources which are naturally replenished by nature. For the right applications this makes them favourable to use over metals and plastics which are mined from ore and oil reserves and use up limited minerals in the earth's crust.

Renewable materials also tend to age more gracefully than synthetic materials, making them more durable and providing more opportunity for consumer attachment and product longevity.

Treeplast is a natural, renewable and biodegradable material made from 50 per cent wood chips, with crushed corn and natural resins, containing no plastics. It comes in a range of different versions including fully biodegradable and water-resistant. It can be finished like wood and has comparable properties to MDF. Its natural appearance provides an interesting communication mechanism. Treeplast can also be extruded to make granulate, which can subsequently be processed in traditional plastic-processing machines, providing an interesting alternative for plastics producers (PV Design and Engineering BV, 2001). (See Figure 4.4).

RECYCLED MATERIAL

Many mainstream materials can and do contain recycled content. While some materials are downgraded into a lower quality material when they are recycled,

Figure 4.4 Treeplast

steel, aluminium and glass can be recycled into high quality material with the same properties as virgin material. Recycled plastics which are processed as high quality waste, by being separated in single material streams and then cleaned prior to recycling can maintain many of the original properties in subsequent uses. Downgraded recycled plastics, from mixed waste streams, can also be effectively and economically specified in the manufacture of hidden components without any loss of quality.

Recycled composites are a potential output of the recycling process. For example, Tectan is a chipboard like material made from recycled Tetrapak drinks cartons. Although composites create important markets for recycled materials it is important to recognise that they are often difficult or impossible to recycle themselves.

HAZARDOUS MATERIALS

It is always advisable to avoid the use of hazardous materials. The introduction of the European RoHS Directive (see Appendix) has led to a ban on the use of certain hazardous substances in electrical and electronic equipment. The subsequent introduction of the WEEE Directive (also outlined in Chapter 3) requires that in addition to the substances banned under RoHS, companies have to ensure that components such as; batteries, printed circuit boards larger than 10 cm^2, toner cartridges, and cathode ray tubes are removed from products before they are disposed of, because of the toxic materials that they contain (see Appendix 1).

VARIETY OF MATERIALS

Although it is often impossible to make a product out of one material (because of the need for friction or cohesion), it is good practice to minimise the number of materials used in a design. Reducing the number of different types of material that you specify will help increase the efficiency of end of life processing prior to recycling. A product or sub assembly which is largely made up of one material will not require as much disassembly at the end of its life as a product which is made up of many different constituent parts.

QUANTITY OF MATERIALS

Reducing the quantity of material used in the manufacture of a product through sensible ribbing design is common good practice which can reduce manufacturing costs and create more efficient manufacturing practices as well as leading to other environmental saving such as:

- reducing waste sent to landfill,
- conserving virgin resources, and
- reducing the volume and weight of the product which reduces costs and conserves resources in transportation.

Impact of Use

For domestic energy using products the use stage has been identified as having significant environmental and social impacts, due to the way that people use their products (Environmental Change Unit, 1997; Sherwin and Bhamra, 1998). For example, the environmental impact of washing is directly related to wash frequency, the size of the load, the cycle selected and the amount of detergent used (Sherwin and Bhamra, 1998). Similarly, the environmental impact of cooking is directly linked to dietary habits (meat eater or vegetarian) and cooking behaviours such as whether saucepans are used with lids, how long the oven is heated either side of cooking, and the number of times the oven door is opened during cooking (Sherwin and Bhamra, 1998).

The use stage is also a stage where designers have the opportunity to directly influence behaviour though lifestyles and consumption. Designers have a great opportunity available to them to educate consumers to behave more responsibly. This can be done taking design-focused approaches or user-focused approaches, or a combination of both.

DESIGN-FOCUSED APPROACHES

Design-focused approaches can determine a range of different issues, such as: the energy source, energy efficiency, dual functionality and the use of consumables.

Energy source

Most conventional consumer goods are battery powered or plug into the mains, drawing their energy from non-renewable fossil fuels. If traditional energy forms are needed, mains power is preferable as this reduces the end of life impact associated with disposing of batteries. However, if batteries must be used there are a number of different types that designers can choose from. Disposable alkaline or lithium batteries are best avoided as they have such a short life span. Nickel Cadmium (NiCad) rechargeable batteries are also best avoided because they contain highly toxic cadmium. The best batteries to use are rechargeable Nickel Metal Hydride (NiMH), rechargeable Lithium Ion or rechargeable alkaline batteries (Datschefski, 2004).

Designers might also consider using renewable energy forms such as kinetic, solar, wind and wave energy. Over the last decade, these forms of power supply have become more widely utilised in a number of key markets such as:

- Emergency equipment – muscle and solar powered torches, radios and mobile phone chargers.
- Outdoor equipment – solar powered heating, lighting, and water fountains.
- Domestic applications – solar powered heating, and solar powered cooking.
- Local council applications – solar powered street lighting in sunny environments.

Although alternative energy moves away from the consumption of fossil fuels and taps into 'free' energy sources, there are potential rebound effects which need to be taken into consideration, such as the ecological impact of solar panels. The best form of powering a product is through muscle power, because there are limited rebound effects (Datschefski, 2004).

Although the advent of the Baygen wind up radio and similar products by Sony and Philips have helped to remove the 'hippy' association with muscle powered products, they still don't have a high 'cool' factor. These issues and the extra inconvenience which is often associated with human-powered products means that the technology may be limited in its application.

Figure 4.5 '**Sunrise**' **outdoor table**

The 'Sunrise' outdoor table design by Ben Manwaring (designed while he was studying at Loughborough University) collects solar energy via 12 solar panels housed in the transparent table top, in conjunction with a charge controller and 12 V battery to store solar energy for evening lighting. The central light is in the 'down' position during the daytime while charging takes places. It is released when required, by pushing down upon the central dome. A central column then rises up via the internal gas strut, and illuminates automatically. Eighteen White LED's are angled to evenly illuminate the tabletop. The system is over specified to work in overcast conditions and on a full day's charge will produce between 6 and 8 hours of illumination (Lofthouse, 2000).

Reproduced with permission © Loughborough University

Energy efficiency

Environmental impacts of the use stage can be reduced through the application of new technologies which increase resource efficiency. This approach is encouraged in part by the introduction of the EU Energy Label. Philips, for example reduced the energy consumption of their standard monitors to among the lowest on the market (Philips, 1999). However, unintended user behaviour, challenges the potential success of technological intervention in reducing the impacts of the use stage (Lilley et al., 2005). The beneficial design changes made to the Philips monitor can be negated if it is permanently left on by the user (Lilley et al., 2005). Similarly, a washing machine with an AA energy rated 40 °C wash setting can be overridden by the user who can still opt for a 90 °C wash.

Dual functionality

Creating a product which combines a range of functions, such as mobile phones which enable users to make calls, surf the Internet, take photographs, and store data, have the potential to reduce the overall environmental impact of the functions being fulfilled if they lead to an overall reduction in the amount of products that a customer purchases. An obvious rebound effect here would be for a consumer to throw out a number of working items because they have been replaced by a new product which includes that functionality. Alternatively, customers may end up with functions that they do not want or need or which are fulfilled better by a product that they already own.

Consumables

Company policy can encourage users to waste more, especially if a heavy focus is placed on the sale of 'consumables'. Actively, limiting the amount of disposable 'consumables' or 'attachments' needed to operate the product can help to reduce this impact. If consumables are required, ensure they are designed to be easily disassembled for recycling or reuse, as is now the case with many types of printer cartridges.

USER-FOCUSED APPROACHES

User-focused approaches are concerned with reducing environmental and social impacts by designing for behavioural change by using approaches such as: eco-feedback, behaviour steering and intelligent products and systems (Lilley et al., 2005). Research has shown that for maximum effectiveness a combination of these approaches is recommended (Lilley, 2007).

Eco-feedback

Eco-feedback is an approach which aims to provide consumers with enough information, through the product, to persuade them to modify their behaviour and make better choices (Lilley et al., 2005). To be effective the provision of *real-time* feedback is critical in ensuring the information provided is integrated into the consumer's decision-making process (McCalley, 2006).

The Kambrook Axis kettle, designed at RMIT in Australia provides a good illustration of how this approach can work (RMIT, 1997). When developing the Axis kettle, a key requirement of the brief was to reduce the amount of energy consumed during use. Having found no suitable technological answer to the problem the design team studied the users' behaviour to see whether this provided any answers to the efficiency problems. The study concluded that users tend to fill the kettle fuller than required, turn the kettle on, walk off to do something, then come back 5 minutes later and reboil the kettle before using the hot water (RMIT, 1997). These findings enabled the designers to identify three new ways of reducing the energy consumption of the kettle. The water gauge was made clearer and moved to the top of the jug. The jug cavity was insulated with a double wall, to keep the water hotter for longer and reduce the energy needed to reboil the kettle. A temperature indicator was fitted so the user could tell whether it was necessary to reboil the kettle (Sweatman and Gertsakis, 1996).

Another great example is the Viridian light switch produced in 2000 for the Viridian design competition (Viridian, 2000). The light switch is a conceptual idea which aims to educate the user, by helping them recognise how much energy they use. The idea is that one press of the switch will allow the light to be switched on for a set length of time. This is communicated to the user as a fingerprint-shaped light on the switch pad. As the time elapses and the energy is consumed, the light fades away. The concept aims to help consumers develop a better understanding of how much energy they use by enabling them to make a connection between energy and time (Lofthouse, 2003).

Although eco-feedback approaches provide consumers with the information to enable them to change their behaviour, information does not necessarily lead to action.

Behaviour steering

'Behaviour steering' or 'scripts' can be used to encourage consumers to behave in certain ways (Jelsma and Knot, 2002). Through the inscription of incentives and rules, desirable behaviours can be encouraged and undesirable ones can be restricted or removed (Jelsma, 2003). After identifying that their customers were using more washing powder than is needed to ensure a good result, Unilever moved away from the traditional powder format to a tablet format to prevent consumers from using excessive amounts of powder. This increased the efficiency of the wash and reduced resource consumption (Unilever, 2001).

Intelligent products and systems

Intelligent products and systems attempt to circumvent rebound effects by mitigating, controlling or blocking inappropriate user behaviour (Lilley et al., 2005). IDEO's 'musical mobile' for example, constrains inappropriate use by forcing the user to play out loud, the tune of the number they want to call (IDEO, 2002). In another study looking specifically at the ways in which a mobile phone could display its embarrassment at being made to behave in an inappropriate way solutions such as automatically switching to speaker phone, terminating the call, shaking, stammering and vibrating were proposed (Lilley, 2006). In the final design the phone displays its embarrassment by emitting a red light which disables functionality for a fixed period, enabling the phone to calm down.

User-focused approaches can either force the user to behave in a more environmentally aware manner, or actively educate consumers to behave more responsibly. Overriding any decision making by the user has the potential to be incredibly effective, although the disadvantage is that this lack of choice can lead to a lack of awareness. The question arises whether it is better to educate the consumer and risk failure or overrule them, gain environmental improvements but encourage naivety (Lilley, 2006).

Length of Life

Identifying the optimal life for a product is another consideration which can influence its overall environmental performance (Cooper, 1994). In most cases, products with a longer life use less materials and energy and the lower levels of manufacturing which result from extended life lead to slower depletion of valuable resources such as oil and copper, less pollution, and less waste usage (Cooper, 1994). Despite this it is fairly common for products to become obsolete before the end of their technical life – either because they are no longer fashionable, they have been superseded by more advanced technology, or they have broken and are uneconomic to repair (Cooper, 1994). Disposability has become a consumer benefit (Mackenzie, 1991). Many goods which used to be designed to last for years are now intended to have only a short lifespan (Mackenzie, 1991).

INCREASING PRODUCT LIFESPAN

Product lifespan, or the 'lifetime' of a product can be extended in a number of ways. Lifetimes can be extended by designing products which can be economically repaired or upgraded to bring the product in line with latest technologies. This is common practice with personal computers where additional RAM and new hardware can be easily added via USB ports. Alternatively, product lifespans can be extended by remanufacturing – restoring used products, or components to a condition similar to that of new products (Lewis et al., 2001) or by passing old working products to the second-hand market for reuse via forums such as Freecycle (www.freecycle.org). Washing machines for example have been seen to last for 8 years with their original purchaser and then a further 6 years with subsequent users (Cooper, 1994).

BENEFITS OF DURABLE PRODUCTS

More durable products which have a longer length of life can also be of benefit to the company producing them. By utilising different business models and selecting to design products which have an extended life, they can reap additional financial benefits. For example, in the case of Xerox, the company chose to hold onto the inherent value in the product by leasing rather than selling their photocopiers. They designed and developed higher specification machines which would last longer and leased out these products to their customers. These approaches also have the added benefits of increased customer loyalty, increased servicing and brand development.

LIMITING LIFE TIME

Finally, it is important to recognise that it is not *always* better to extend a product's life – as can be demonstrated in the case of refrigerators. Due to tightened legislative requirements and the introduction of Energy Labelling fridges which have been produced in the last few five years have a much lower energy consumption level than those manufactured 20 years ago. As such it is often actually more environmentally beneficial to dispose of the old fridge, and manufacture a new one than to keep the old fridge in service, because of the differences in running efficiency.

There are other times when it can be opportune to deliberately design short lifespans into a product for the benefit of the environment. For example, some products such as plastic carrier bags and milk cartons, only require a short lifespan.

End of Life

Designing products so that they can be handled responsibly at the end of their life has always been a key focus of the environmental design movement. In recent years, this issue has been given increased importance on the political agenda, due to the introduction of the WEEE Directive (see Chapter 3 for an overview of this legislation) which focuses specifically on electrical and electronic products, advocates four strategies for processing end of life waste; remanufacture, component reuse, recycling and energy recovery. In order to process electronic waste (e-waste) it must first be disassembled to avoid any contamination issues.

DISASSEMBLY

There are four different types of disassembly:
- Mechanical Disassembly
- Automated Disassembly
- Manual Disassembly
- Active Disassembly.

When designing for disassembly the key is to identify the anticipated mode of disposal for the product during the early design stages and build in mechanisms which enable this to happen quickly and easily.

Mechanical disassembly

Mechanical disassembly involves either:

- Shredding/Fragmenting – grinding the product into small pieces which are separated into ferrous metals (iron, steel and nickel), mixed heavies (non-ferrous metals) and waste; or

- Granulating – a size-reduction process used for production scrap, post-consumer plastic packaging, industrial parts, or other materials that must be downsized for further processing.

Automated disassembly

Automated disassembly is only cost-effective where large volumes of the same or very similar products are available for disassembly. It involves using a production line and automated machinery to separate those parts or materials previously identified for reuse or recycling. If automated disassembly is to be used then designers should consider carefully the type of fasteners used within the product. In particular fasteners should be minimised in number to reduce the amount of fasteners, removal of which is often difficult and time consuming. In addition it is essential that fasteners are easily reversible to enable the automatic machinery to remove them.

Manual disassembly

Manual disassembly is used in a variety of contexts from removing hazardous materials at the start of an automated disassembly processing, removing parts for reuse or recycling, through to disassembly to replace failed parts or upgrade the product. It is more expensive than automated disassembly for high volume similar products but more flexible for diverse low-volume products as it can result in a higher yield of useful materials or components.

Manual disassembly can be made much more cost-effective by integrating various mechanisms into the substructure of the product. These mechanisms include (Goldberg, 2000):

- Fixings such as snap fits, clip fits, push fits rather than permanent fixings.

- Hazardous parts grouped together on subassemblies which can be easily removed with the minimal procedure.
- Reduction in the number of parts.
- Easily accessible, visible and clearly marked fastenings points.
- Use of simple component orientation.
- Minimise the amount of force required to remove part to speed up disassembly.
- Use a simple product structure.
- Make sure disassembly points obvious.

Active disassembly

Active Disassembly aims to automate or semi-automate the disassembly process through the use of Smart Materials such as Shape Memory Alloys (SMA) and Shape Memory Polymers (SMP) which can change shape or size at a range of transition temperatures and thus facilitate the release of parts. The range of 'trigger temperatures' for various smart materials means that it is possible to place the products in a heated environment where the outer elements become detached and then move on to a higher temperature zone where internal parts and sub-assemblies are dismantled.

The use of Smart Materials in disassembly could ultimately make the disassembly process much more cost effective, by speeding up the yield of high value components and enabling different products to be disassembled in the same facility (Chiodo et al., 2000). Research into the active disassembly of mobile phones resulted in a mean disassembly time of just over 8 seconds, and in these cases disassembly was achieved without any damage to the host product (Chiodo and Boks, 2002). It is likely that active disassembly will be most useful for products which have components with a high intrinsic value such as Mobile phones and IT equipment (for more detail see the Nokia case study in Chapter 6).

REMANUFACTURING

Remanufacturing is the process of restoring used products, or components, to a condition that has similar performance characteristics to new products (Lewis et al., 2001). This extends the life of products and promotes the re-use of components and materials. It generally involves five stages: manual disassembly, cleaning, re-assembly, parts refurbishment and testing.

Remanufacturing is a popular approach for products such as photocopiers, power tools, vacuum cleaners and garden and leisure equipment, where the effects of fashion changes are minimal. It is, however, rarely used for domestic products because of the rapid changes in styling and technology associated with these types of product; the decentralised and unpredictable supply for used goods; the high transport costs; and the customer prejudice against rebuilt products (Henstock, 1988; Lewis et al., 2001).

COMPONENT REUSE

Reusing your own or someone else's components can be a cost-effective strategy for reducing the impact of a product at the end of its life and is especially useful for high value or durable components and unseen, static parts. Component reuse is usually only possible if it has been identified in the early stage of the design of the product, so that certain approaches can be taken into consideration. For example, parts which have been identified for reuse need to be integrated into the design with flexible fixings which allows them to be easily and safely removed without damage. It will also be important to understand the expected lifespan of the components that are to be reused and how this will be monitored. Consideration will have to be given to how to get the components back for reuse, how many components will be available per month/year, how parts will be cleaned and tested before it is reused and, finally, how they will be integrated into existing manufacturing processes. The Kodak case study in Chapter 6 provides a great example of how this can be carried out successfully.

RECYCLING

Recycling is the recovery of materials or components from products for processing. The recycling of metals has been an established process for many years. It is generally done through one of two methods: shredding and separation to recover both ferrous and non ferrous metals, and disassembly and recycling to recover metals and some other materials. Plastics recycling is not as well established.

Rising volumes and diversity of plastic content in e-waste means that understanding how to recycle plastics is becoming an area of great interest (Fisher et al., 2005). Plastics can be recovered using a variety of technologies.

- The mechanical recycling of plastics involves melting, shredding and granulation of waste plastics. Plastics must be sorted prior to mechanical recycling into polymer types and/or colour. The plastic is then melted down directly and moulded into a new shape or melted down after being shredded into flakes and then processed into granules called regranulate.

- Chemical or feedstock recycling is plastic recovery which breaks polymers down into their constituent monomers which in turn can be used again in refineries or petrochemical or chemical production. This process can tolerate greater levels of impurities than mechanical recycling but is capital intensive and requires very large quantities of used plastic to be economically viable (50,000 tonnes per year) (Waste on Line, 2004).

Some components such as PCBs, batteries, CRT require specialist recycling. Many PCBs found in e-waste have a low intrinsic value and therefore are not economic to recycle. Generally, only those found in IT and telecommunications equipment have any intrinsic value. These can be processed to recover materials such as: silver, lead, copper, and gold using a process called Pyrolytic treatment (smelting) which extracts the precious metals from the boards.

To facilitate recycling there are many different labelling systems for different types of products and materials. Appendix 2 outlines the various requirements for plastics, packaging and electrical and electronic products.

ENERGY RECOVERY

Energy recovery is the process by which a product/component is incinerated in order to recapture its energy (European Environment Agency, 2006). However under the WEEE Directive energy recovery is usually only allowable for a small proportion of the weight of the product and it is important to recognise that some materials need treating before they can be sent for energy recovery. Energy recovery is an economically and environmentally viable approach to dealing with the recovery of plastics resulting from e-waste and is preferable to landfill (Fisher et al., 2005).

Needs

In the 1980s Papanek recognised that:

> *'Much recent design has satisfied only evanescent wants and desires, while the genuine needs of man have often been neglected. The economic, psychological, spiritual, social, technological, and intellectual needs of a human being are usually more difficult and less profitable to satisfy than the carefully engineered and manipulated "wants" inculcated by fad and fashion.'*

(Papanek, 1985, p. 15)

Asking whether a product is actually needed should be a core concern of the responsible designer. The profession of industrial design was born out of an inter-war American economic system which was becoming increasingly dependent on encouraging high consumption levels to create wealth (Whiteley, 1994). Focusing on needs rather than wants is therefore generally incongruous with the role that industrial designers tend to fulfil in modern society – that of meeting consumer demand or industry requirements by fulfilling a proposed brief. However, by encouraging designers to ask where their skills are actually needed rather than focusing purely on market driven requirements we can make sure that we are addressing our responsibility.

In 1970s the designer and visionary Victor Papanek was trying to encourage designers to design for people's needs rather than wants (Papanek, 1971). He identified six priorities for design (Papanek, 1985):

1. Design for the Developing World.
2. Design of Teaching and Training devices for the Retarded, the Handicapped and the Disabled.
3. Design for Medicine, Surgery, Dentistry and Hospital Equipment.
4. Design for Experimental Research.
5. Systems Design for Sustaining Human Life under Marginal Conditions.
6. Design for Breakthrough Concepts.

Twenty years on, these still form a good basis upon which designers can assess the validity of the work that they undertake. They can also help designers to recognise the wide range of ways in which their skill can be utilised.

ADDRESSING HUMAN NEEDS

A number of commentators have reflected on and tried to categorise human needs. Maslow generated a hierarchy of human needs, through which he argued that 'deficiency' needs such as hunger and thirst must be met before 'growth' needs such as self-fulfilment can be met (see Table 4.2) (Maslow, 1971; Maslow and Lowery, 1998, Huitt, 2004).

Table 4.2   Summary of Maslow's hierarchy of needs

Deficiency needs	Physiological	Hunger, thirst, bodily comforts
	Safety/security	Out of danger
	Belonginess and Love	Affiliate with others, be accepted
	Esteem	To achieve, be competent, gain approval and recognition
Growth needs	Cognitive	To know, to understand, explore
	Aesthetic	Symmetry, order, beauty
	Self-actualisation	To find self-fulfillment and realise one's potential
	Self-transcendence	To connect to something beyond the ego or to help others find self-fulfillment and realise their potential

Max-Neef (1992), avoided a hierarchical interpretation of needs by identifying nine fundamental needs: Subsistence, Protection, Affection, Understanding, Participation, Leisure, Creation, Identity, Freedom – which are associated with four states of existence: being, having, doing and interacting (see Table 4.3).

Max-Neef argues that fundamental needs remain constant across time and culture; what changes is the ways in which these needs are satisfied. Only two of these needs require material means to satisfy them – subsistence and protection, yet in industrialised countries we attempt to satisfy them all through material means. He believes each of these needs are always present and that they are not substitutable, though through our selection of satisfiers we can fulfil more than one need at once. Max-Neef (1992) devised five different types of satisfier:

- Singular-satisfiers satisfy one need and are neutral in the satisfaction of others. For example, welfare programmes to provide housing provide subsistence, and the giving of gifts provides affection.

- Synergic-satisfiers satisfy a given need, and stimulate or contribute to the simultaneous satisfaction of other needs. For example, education – satisfies the need for understanding – while also satisfying the need for protection, participation, creation, identity and freedom.

- Pseudo-satisfiers stimulate a false sense of satisfaction, in the way that fashion fulfils the need for identify.

- Inhibitors satisfy one need but impair the possibility of other needs being met. For example, it could be said that television satisfies the need for leisure but impairs understanding, creation and identity.

- Violators do not satisfy the need supposed to be satisfied and annihilate other needs being satisfied. For example, censorship is supposed to provide protection, but actually inhibits understanding, participation, leisure creation, identity and freedom.

The needs identified by Max-Neef (see Table 4.3) can be used by design teams to reframe the brief so that the focus moves away from a product-focused orientation. They can also be used to evaluate a new product idea to determine how valuable it is.

Conclusions

This chapter has argued that because of their position in the product development process, designers have an innate responsibility to ensure that negative environmental and social impacts are minimised. It has shown how designers can improve the environmental and social impact of the products they design by focusing on improving the impacts of different stages of the product life cycle or by concentrating on meeting human needs. It has demonstrated that there are two different ways of approaching design for sustainability, by focusing on the product life cycle or by focusing on needs. Both are valuable approaches, with different advantages and limitations.

The life cycle approach, is compatible with current product development, which means it can and is being taken up by industry. Current industrial practice tends to focus on reducing the impact of the product life cycle and can lead to incremental improvements in either an environmental and/or social dimension. Environmental improvements might include using less material and creating less impact from transport. Whereas social improvements might include increasing local sourcing and active encouragement of employees donating a percentage of their working time to charity, these small positive changes can have significant positive environmental and social impacts when they are multiplied by the amount of products produced *per annum*. For example, reducing the weight of a portable television from 9.5 kg to 9 kg will create a saving of 50,000 kg of material for 100,000 units. This will have positive environmental implications on the overall footprint of the product, reducing the impact of the mining required for the virgin materials, reducing transportation costs and reducing the amount of material which will eventually go to landfill if the television has not been

Table 4.3   Max-Neef's satisfiers of human needs (Max-Neef, 1992)

Fundamental Human Needs	Being (qualities)	Having (things)	Doing (actions)	Interacting (settings)
Subsistence	physical & mental health	food, shelter, work	feed, clothe, rest, work	living environment, social setting
Protection	care, adaptability, autonomy	social security, health systems, work	co-operate, plan, take care of, help	social environment, dwelling
Affection	respect, sense of humour, generosity, sensuality	friendships, family, relationships with nature	share, take care of, make love, express emotions	privacy, intimate spaces of togetherness
Understanding	critical capacity, curiosity, intuition	literature, teachers, policies educational	analyse, study, meditate investigate	schools, families, universities, communities
Participation	receptiveness, dedication, sense of humour	responsibilities, duties, work, rights	co-operate, dissent, express opinions	associations, parties, churches, neighbourhoods
Leisure	imagination, tranquillity, spontaneity	games, parties, peace of mind	day-dream, remember, relax, have fun	landscapes, intimate spaces, places to be alone
Creation	imagination, boldness, inventiveness, curiosity	abilities, skills, work, techniques	invent, build, design, work, compose, interpret	spaces for expression, workshops, audiences
Identity	sense of belonging, self-esteem, consistency	language, religions, work, customs, values, norms	get to know oneself, grow, commit oneself	places one belongs to, everyday settings
Freedom	autonomy, passion, self-esteem, open-mindedness	equal rights	dissent, choose, run risks, develop awareness	anywhere

designed for end of life processing. However, the life cycle approach tends to encourage designers to think within the current paradigm.

The other approach is a needs-focused approach, where the customer's needs are central to the brief. This is what marketers would argue currently happens with market-driven design. We would strongly argue that the current paradigm is actually consumption-driven design and not needs orientated. Taking a needs focus encourages new ways of thinking but is in many ways at odds with the capitalist model in which most western designers work. For a needs-focused approach to be established within industry, it would have to be recognised at a strategic level.

References

Chiodo, J. D. and Boks, C. (2002), 'Assessment of End-of-Life Strategies with Active Disassembly Using Smart Materials', *Journal of Sustainable Product Design*, 2, pp. 69–82. [DOI: 10.1023/B%3AJSPD.0000016422.01386.7c].

Chiodo, J. D., McLaren, J., Billet, E. H. and Harrison, D. J. (2000), 'Isolating LCD's at End-of-Life Using Active Disassembly Technology: A Feasibility Study', presented at IEEE International Symposium on Electronics and the Environment, San Francisco, CA.

Cooper, T. (1994) 'Beyond Recycling?' *Eco Design*, **3**:2.

Datschefski, E. (2004), 'Materials Choice'. Available at: www.biothinking.com/materials.htm

European Environment Agency (2006) EEA Glossary. Available at: http://glossary.eea.europa.eu/EEAGlossary/E/energy_recovery

Environmental Change Unit (1997), *2MtC – DECADE: Domestic Equipment and Carbon Dioxide Emissions* (Oxford: Oxford University Press).

Fabrycky, W. J. (1987), 'Designing for the Life Cycle', *Mechanical Engineering*, January, pp. 72–74.

Fisher, M., Frank, M., Kingsbury, T., Vehlow, J. and Yamawaki, T. (2005), 'Energy Recovery in the Sustainable Recycling of Plastics from End-of-Life Electrical and Electronic Products', presented at IEEE International Symposium on Electronics and the Environment (2005 ISEE/SUMMIT), New Orleans, LA.

Friedman, T. L. (2005), 'Global is Good', *The Guardian* 21st April 2005.

Goldberg, L. H. (2000), *Green Electronics/Green Bottom Line: Environmentally Responsible Engineering*, ISBN: 0750699930 (Massachusetts: Newnes).

Henstock, M. E. (1988), *Design for Recyclability* (London: The Institute of Metals).

Huitt, W. (2004), 'Maslow's Hierarchy of Needs', *Educational Psychology Interactive*. Available at: http://chiron.valdosta.edu/whuitt/col/regsys/maslow.html (Valdosta, GA: Valdosta State University).

IDEO (2002), *Social Mobiles,* (London: IDEO).

Jelsma, J. (2003), 'Innovating for Sustainability: Involving Users, Politics and Technology', *Innovation*, 16, pp. 103–116.

Jelsma, J. and Knot, M. (2002), 'Designing Environmentally Efficient Services; a 'script' Approach', *The Journal of Sustainable Product Design*, 2, pp. 119–130. [DOI: 10.1023/B%3AJSPD.0000031031.20974.1b].

Koninklijke Philips Electronics N.V. (1999), *Greening Your Business* (Eindhoven: Koninklijke Philips Electronics N.V.).

Lewis, H., Gertsakis, J., Grant, T., Morelli, N. and Sweatman, A. (2001), *Design + Environment, a Global Guide to Designing Greener Goods* (Sheffield: Greenleaf Publishing).

Lilley, D. (2006), 'Designing for Behavioural Change' *Engage Newsletter*, May, pp. 4–9. Available at: www.designandemotion.org/society/engage/newsletters.html

Lilley, D. (2007), 'Towards Sustainable Use: An Exploration of Design for Behavioural Change', Doctoral Thesis, Department of Design Technology (Loughborough: Loughborough University).

Lilley, D., Lofthouse, V. A. and Bhamra, T. A. (2005), 'Towards Instinctive Sustainable Product Use', presented at 2nd International Conference in Sustainability Creating the Culture, Aberdeen, UK.

Lofthouse, V. A. (2000), *Information/Inspiration* (Cranfield: Cranfield University).

Lofthouse, V. A. (2003), 'Information/Inspiration', Available at: www.informationinspiration.org.uk (Loughborough: Loughborough University).

Mackenzie, D. (1991), *Green Design: Design for the Environment* (London: Laurence King Publishing Ltd.).

Maslow, A. (1971), *The Farther Reaches of Human Nature* (New York: The Viking Press).

Maslow, A. and Lowery, R. (1998), *Toward a Psychology of Being* (New York: Wiley and Sons).

Max-Neef, M. A. (1992), 'From the Outside Looking' In *Experiences in 'Barefoot Economics'* (London: Zed Books).

McCalley, L. T. (2006), 'From Motivation and Cognition Theories to Everyday Applications and Back Again: The Case of Product-Integrated Information and Feedback', *Energy Policy*, 34, pp. 129–137. [DOI: 10.1016/j.enpol.2004.08.024].

Papanek, V. (1971), *Design for the Real World* (New York: Pantheon Books).

Papanek, V. (1985), *Design for the Real World: Human Ecology and Social Change* (London: Thames & Hudson).

PV Design and Engineering BV (2001), 'What is Treeplast?'. Available at: www.treeplast.com/what_is_treeplast.htm

RMIT (1997), *Introduction to EcoReDesign – Improving the Environmental Performance of Manufactured Products* (Melbourne, Victoria: Royal Melbourne Institute of Technology).

Sherwin, C. and Bhamra, T. (1998), 'Ecodesign Innovation: Present Concepts, Current Practice and Future Directions for Design and the Environment', presented at Design History Society Conference, University of Huddersfield, UK.

Smith, L. and Henderson, M. (2006), 'TV Standby Buttons Will Be Outlawed' In *The Times On-Line,* 12th July 2006.

Sweatman, A. and Gertsakis, J. (1996), 'Eco-Kettle: Keep the Kettle Boiling', *Co-Design*, 05/06, p. 3.

Unilever (2001), 'Dose: A Sustainable Step for Fabrics Liquids' prepared and issued by Unilever HPC – Europe.

University of Warwick (2004), 'Researchers Compost Old Mobile Phones and Transform Them into Flowers'. Available at: www2.warwick.ac.uk/newsandevents/pressreleases/NE1000000097300/

Methods and Tools for Design for Sustainability

CHAPTER 5

The challenge for designers is to find meaningful tools which engage with the design process and help them to tackle design for sustainability (Lofthouse, 2004). Rather than providing an exhaustive list of the tools available, this chapter introduces a selection of those which have proved to be relevant to design students and practising designers alike. They are grouped into five sections (see Figure 5.1):

- Environmental Assessment
- Strategic Design
- Idea generation
- User centred design and
- Information provision.

Environmental Assessment Tools

Environmental assessment tools are quantitative tools which tend to be most useful at the early stages of the product development process where they can be used to evaluate an existing design and identify opportunities for improvement. They are useful for benchmarking against competitors and making comparisons between products which have similar functions, for example CD player and MP3 Player. This section introduces and reflects on three different tools: Life Cycle Assessment, the MET Matrix and the Eco-Indicator 99.

LIFE CYCLE ASSESSMENT TOOLS

Life Cycle Assessment (LCA), as the name implies, is a methodology for assessing the environmental impacts of a product (or service) from the initial extraction and processing of raw materials to final disposal – from 'cradle to grave' (Ayres, 1995). LCA is a time consuming, expensive, scientific approach which in many cases does not offer a clear-cut answer (Ayres, 1995). The problem arises in

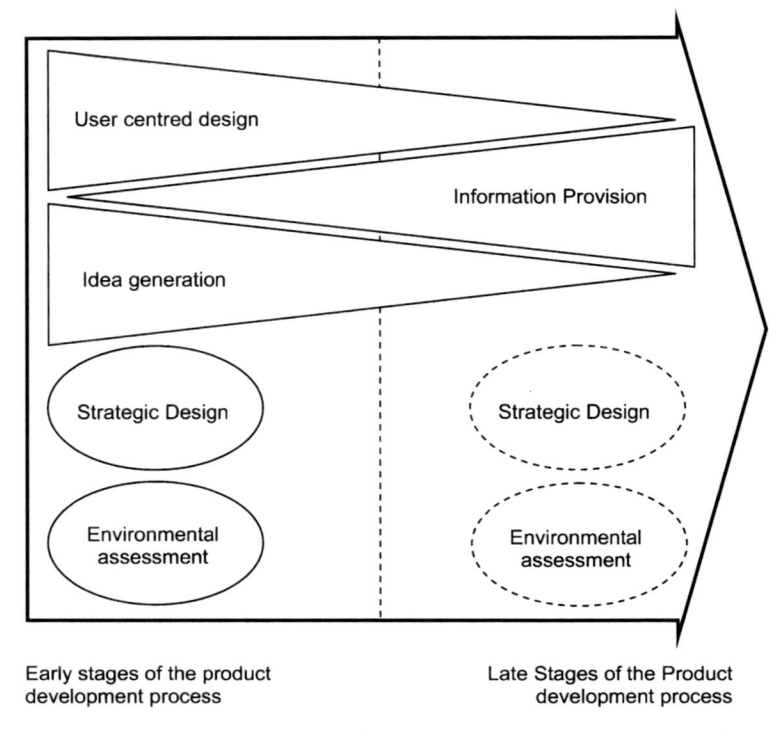

Figure 5.1 Design for sustainability methods and tools mapped across the product development process

part, from the difficulty of comparing products with completely different eco-profiles. For example, it has been estimated that, although polystyrene cups take up more space in landfill than paper cups, paper cups require 36 times more electricity and 580 times more wastewater to manufacture. In addition to this, when paper cups are sent to landfill they eventually degrade anaerobically, generating methane (Hocking, 1991; Ayres, 1995).

It is also very difficult to set the exact system boundary that will form part of the assessment. For example, when assessing a photocopier should you include the toner and paper used during life and therefore the impact of their manufacturing process as well? Other problems with LCA include the fact that data is very difficult to access and often average data from many different countries and manufacturing faculties is used which can mean that there is a lack of accuracy.

Although it is not recommended for designers to carry out an LCA, because of the time involved, when they are conclusive, the results can be useful to inform the design process. For example, an LCA of domestic products identified

> **Reusable cloth nappies vs. disposable paper nappies**
>
> Many assessments have been undertaken over the years to identify which is better for the environment. Disposable nappies create 90 times more solid waste than reusable nappies (but this is only 2 per cent of total municipal waste), whereas reusable cloth nappies generate 10 times as much water pollution (including detergents) and consume 3 times as much energy as disposable nappies (Ayres, 1995). However, reusable nappies have a long lifetime and can be used for more than one child. This argument is currently unresolved, which illustrates how difficult it is to interpret the results of LCA.

that the use phase of washing machines and cookers is more environmentally damaging than the manufacturing and disposal stages (Environmental Change Unit, 1997). This suggests that it is more valuable for producers to focus on reducing the impact of the use phase, rather than being preoccupied with manufacture and disposal. Similarly an LCA carried out by Nokia identified that one of the greatest environmental impacts of a mobile phone is caused by the amount of energy used by the product and charger under normal conditions (Nokia, 2005).

MET MATRIX

The MET Matrix is an abridged LCA tool which can be useful at the beginning of the design process. It was developed by researchers at Delft University in the Netherlands specifically to help designers understand the environmental problems associated with products they were redesigning (Brezet and van Hemel, 1997). MET stands for Materials, Energy and Toxicity and represents the three areas examined through the matrix.

Using an empty MET matrix (as illustrated in Table 5.1) the product analysis starts by considering the implications of each cell of the matrix ensuring that issues associated with any auxiliary materials are considered, as well as the product itself. For example, a MET Matrix of a photocopier would also consider toner and paper.

In each matrix cell notes about any environmental problems should be recorded. The materials column is intended for notes on environmental problems associated with both the input and output of materials across the life cycle. It should be used to record quantities of materials which are:

- non renewable;
- likely to create emissions during production;

Table 5.1 MET Matrix

		Materials Cycle Input/output	Energy Use Input/output	Toxic Emissions
Production and supply of materials & components				
In-house production				
Distribution				
Utilisation	operation			
	servicing			
End of life system	recovery			
	disposal			

- incompatible from a recycling perspective;
- inefficient in their use;
- not suitable for reuse of materials.

The energy use column should quantify energy consumption during all life cycle stages. The toxic emissions column should be used to record all toxic emissions to land, water and air across all life cycle stages.

This tool can be used in two ways, initially it gives a quick qualitative overview of potential environmental problems. It can then be followed up with a more detailed, quantitative evaluation of exactly how much waste is produced or material is mined for example. Because it examines the three main areas associated with environmental problems it enables trade-offs to be made during the design process. For example, a designer may select a part to be made from a new material which is heavier than the previous generation if it results in less emissions during production or use.

Once the redesign is complete the product can be reassessed to get a picture of the overall improvements achieved. Table 5.2 illustrates a completed MET matrix for a coffee vending machine.

Table 5.2 Example of a completed MET Matrix for a coffee vending machine

		Materials Cycle Input/output	Energy Use Input/output	Toxic Emissions
Production and supply of materials & components		• Copper • Zinc	• High energy content of materials	• Fire retardants in printed circuit boards • Flow improvers – injection moulding • PS: benzene emissions • PUR: isocyanate • Emissions due to painting and gluing
In-house production		• Metal waste • Plastic waste	• Process energy	
Distribution				
Utilisation	operation	• Plastic cups (1.472 kg PS) • Filter paper (90 kg) • Plastic spoons (110 kg PP) • Cleaning materials • Polluted waste (4 l) • Water filters 20)	• Inefficient energy use by boiler • Transport energy	
	servicing	• Easily broken parts	• Transport of service providers	
End of life system	recovery	• No reuse of valuable parts such as boiler • Disposal of coffee machine (37 kg) • Packaging • No recycling of plastics • Plastics (5 kg) • Print plates (0.5 kg)		
	disposal			• Printed circuit boards (0.5 kg) • Copper • Zinc

ECO-INDICATOR 99

Eco-Indicator 99, created by Pré Consultants in The Netherlands, is a practical impact assessment tool which allows designers to calculate the environmental impacts of a product or design. The tool and all the associated worksheets can be downloaded for free from www.pre.nl. Eco-Indicator 99 allows teams to calculate standard indicator scores for frequently used materials and processes.

Designers carrying out the analysis are encouraged to produce a list of component parts by disassembling the product and identifying the materials and processes that make up each part. Each element is added to the correct section on the table and quantified in relevant units (for example, raw materials in kilograms, electricity in kilowatt hours, and transport in tonnes per kilometre). The next stage is to look up the Eco-indicator value for each product element from the tables provided. The Eco-indicator value is a representation of the impact of the product element based on its effect on human health, ecosystem quality and resource use. The weight of each of the product elements is multiplied by the Eco-indicator value to give the eco-points. The higher the points, the worse the environmental impact of that element. The total number of eco-points can then be calculated for each life cycle stage. Table 5.3 shows a completed Eco-Indicator 99 table for an electric juicer.

Table 5.3   Completed Eco-Indicator 99 for an electric juicer

Production				
Material or process		Amount (kg)	Indicator	Result
Polystyrene (PS)		0.1	370	37
High Density Polyethylene (HDPE)		0.308	330	101.6
Low-Density Polyethylene (LDPE)		0.22	360	79.2
Polyvinyl chloride (PVC)		0.174	240	41.8
Nylon		0.004	240	0.96
Rubber		0.002	360	0.72
Steel		0.010	86	0.86
Copper		0.032	1400	44.8
Cardboard		0.150	69	10.35
Paper		0.01	96	0.96
Injection moulding − 1		0.41	21	8.61
Injection moulding − 2	(PVC)	0.174	44	7.66
TOTAL				**334.52**

Table 5.3 *Concluded*

Use		Amount (kg)	Indicator	Result
Electricity (kWh)		1.217	33	40.2
Shipping of product (tkm) 1.1/1000 × 11,000		12.1 tkm	1.1	13.31
Distribution (tkm) 1.1/1000 × 200		0.22 tkm	15	3.3
Transport of oranges (tkm) (0.57 × 365 × 5)/1,000 × 1500		1560	15	23,400
TOTAL				**23,456.8**
Disposal		**Amount (kg)**	**Indicator**	**Result**
Landfill				
Polystyrene (PS)		0.1	4.1	0.41
High Density Polyethylene (HDPE)		0.308	3	0.924
Low-Density Polyethylene (LDPE)		0.22	3	0.66
Polyvinyl chloride (PVC)		0.742	2.8	2.078
Nylon		0.004	3.6	0.014
Steel		0.010	1.4	0.014
Copper		0.032	1.4	0.045
Recycling				
Cardboard		0.150	− 8.3	− 1.245
Paper		0.01	− 1.2	− 0.012
TOTAL				**2.88**

Once the redesign is complete the product can be reassessed to get a picture of the overall improvements achieved.

Strategic Design Tools

Strategic design tools are very useful at the early stages of the product development process and at the late stages of the product development process for re-evaluation once improvements have been made. They provide a quick way of identifying which areas are most important to focus. This section introduces four strategic design tools which have proven to be useful resources for a range of different design teams; Ecodesign web, Design Abacus, Five Focal areas and six rules of thumb.

ECODESIGN WEB

Ecodesign Web is a quick and easy tool which helps designers to qualitatively assess a product or design to identify the key areas which they need to focus on. It is an adaptation of The LiDS wheel, developed by the authors in response to the need for a simplified, effective tool. It can be downloaded from the tools section of www.informationinspiration.org.uk.

The Ecodesign Web works by comparing the seven design areas with each other to identify a 'better than' / 'worse than' output. Using the template in Figure 5.2 designers work through the seven sections of the web estimating how good or bad the selected product is in that area. The estimated rating should be marked on the web with a cross. When the activity is complete, the crosses should be joined together, and the shape created will illustrate which areas need the most attention. Figure 5.3 presents a completed Ecodesign web for the isotonic drink shown to the side. In this case 'end of life' and optimal life' are identified as areas to focus on. The Ecodesign web can be carried out again to compare new ideas against the original. Figure 5.4 presents a redesign concept for the Boots Isotonic drink and its associated Ecodesign Web. The web can be used:

- By groups or individuals.
- At the beginning of a design project to assess the environmental performance of an existing product.
- To assess design ideas.
- To help improve ideas and products.
- To draw comparison with competitors products.

DESIGN ABACUS

The original Design Abacus was created by Shot in the Dark and can be accessed in full from www.shotinthedark.co.uk. The method described here has been abridged by the authors and can be completed within a couple of hours. The adapted version can be downloaded from the tools section of www.informationinspiration.org.uk.

The Design Abacus helps designers to assess the sustainability performance of a current product, highlight the areas where further research is needed and outline the targets for their redesign. It can be used at the early design stages to analyse the performance of an existing product or to compare a number

ECODESIGN WEB

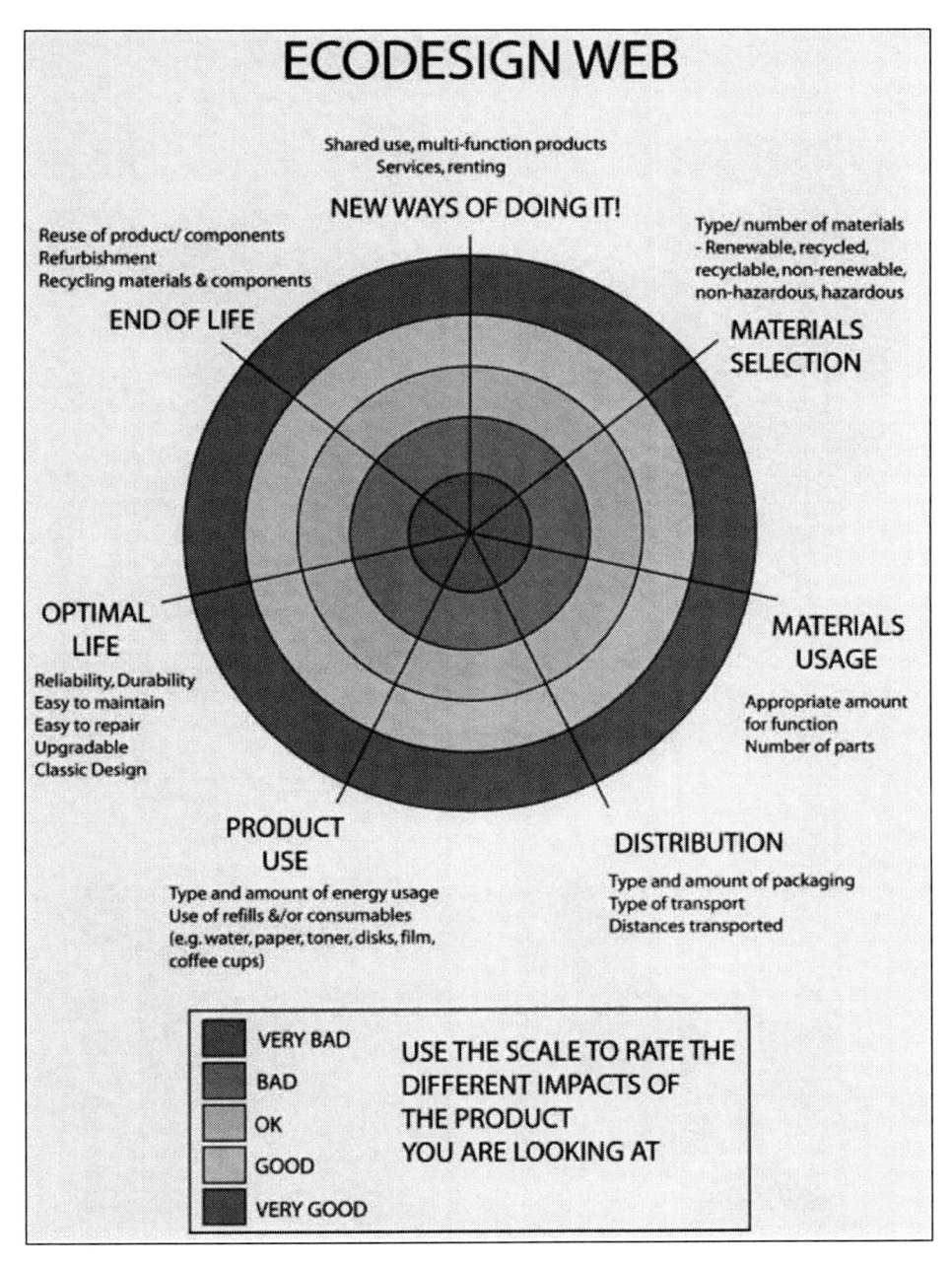

NEW WAYS OF DOING IT!
Shared use, multi-function products
Services, renting

END OF LIFE
Reuse of product/ components
Refurbishment
Recycling materials & components

MATERIALS SELECTION
Type/ number of materials
– Renewable, recycled, recyclable, non-renewable, non-hazardous, hazardous

OPTIMAL LIFE
Reliability, Durability
Easy to maintain
Easy to repair
Upgradable
Classic Design

MATERIALS USAGE
Appropriate amount for function
Number of parts

PRODUCT USE
Type and amount of energy usage
Use of refills &/or consumables
(e.g. water, paper, toner, disks, film, coffee cups)

DISTRIBUTION
Type and amount of packaging
Type of transport
Distances transported

- VERY BAD
- BAD
- OK
- GOOD
- VERY GOOD

USE THE SCALE TO RATE THE DIFFERENT IMPACTS OF THE PRODUCT YOU ARE LOOKING AT

Figure 5.2 Ecodesign Web

Reproduced with permission © Loughborough University

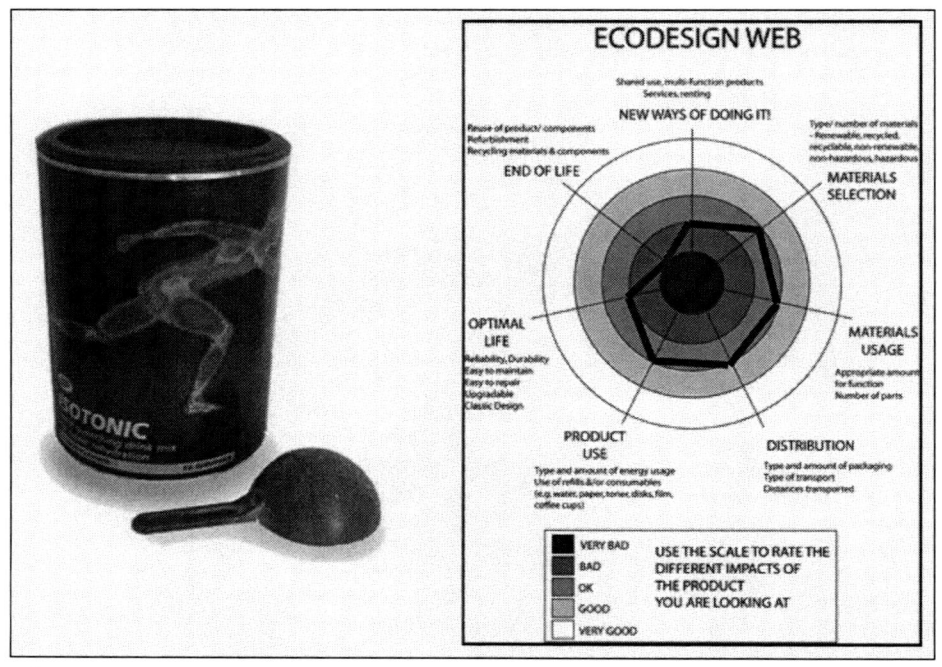

Figure 5.3 Completed Ecodesign web for Boots Isotonic drink
Reproduced with permission © Loughborough University

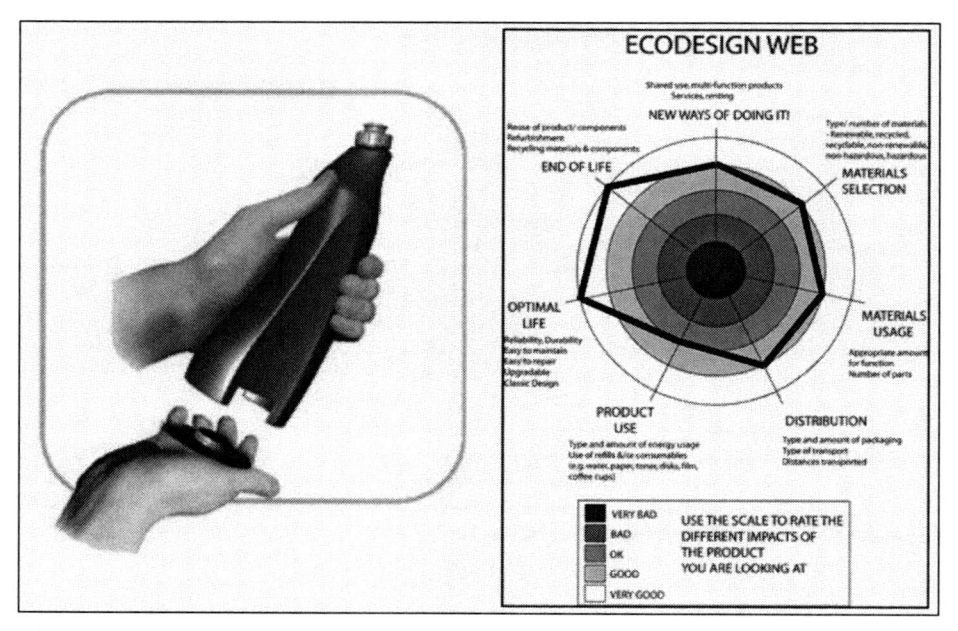

Figure 5.4 Completed Ecodesign web for a new Isotonic drink bottle concept
Reproduced with permission © Loughborough University

of alternative design solutions. It can also be used at the later stages of the development process to make detailed comparison against other designs.

Using the Design Abacus illustrated in Figure 5.5, designers can evaluate a product against specific criteria, grouped under three focal areas which cover a range of different issues – environment (energy, materials, use, end of life, packaging), social/ethical (equity, needs and rights, fairness, equality, ethics, community) and economics (cost, quality, aesthetics, ergonomics). To carry out the activity, designers need at least one copy of the Abacus for each focal area. The area being focused on, for example Environment, is written in the 'FOCAL AREA' box. For each focal area, a number of issues need to be identified and each issue needs to be represented as both a good and bad characteristic. For example, if 'energy use' is the issue, a good characteristic is 'no energy use' and a bad characteristic is 'high energy use'. Other examples include:

- Environment – single material/many different materials, high recycled content/low recycled content, easy to disassembly/difficult to disassembly, long life/short life, high number of recyclable materials/no recyclable materials, no packaging/many levels of packaging.
- Social/ethical – produced locally/produced overseas.
- Economic – high cost of materials/low cost of materials.

To assess the product, each issue should be considered in turn and a judgement made on how the product performs in this area. This is just a relative measure and accuracy is not needed. Once the score (+ 2, + 1, 0, – 1 or – 2) is assigned for a particular issue the level of confidence in this assumption should then be indicated on the top grid. This helps to highlight areas where further research about the product is needed before a final score can be assigned. The assessment continues until all issues have been considered.

The individual sheets are then joined together and a line drawn to connect all the scores and confidence levels (see Figure 5.6). This assessment then gives a visual result that highlights the good and bad areas of the product. The targets for the redesign can then be drawn on the abacus in a different colour and when the redesign is complete it can be assessed against the target to see if it has been met.

FAST FIVE

Philips use an approach called 'Fast five' as a quick mechanism for analysing products without the need for calculation (Philips Corporate Design, 1996).

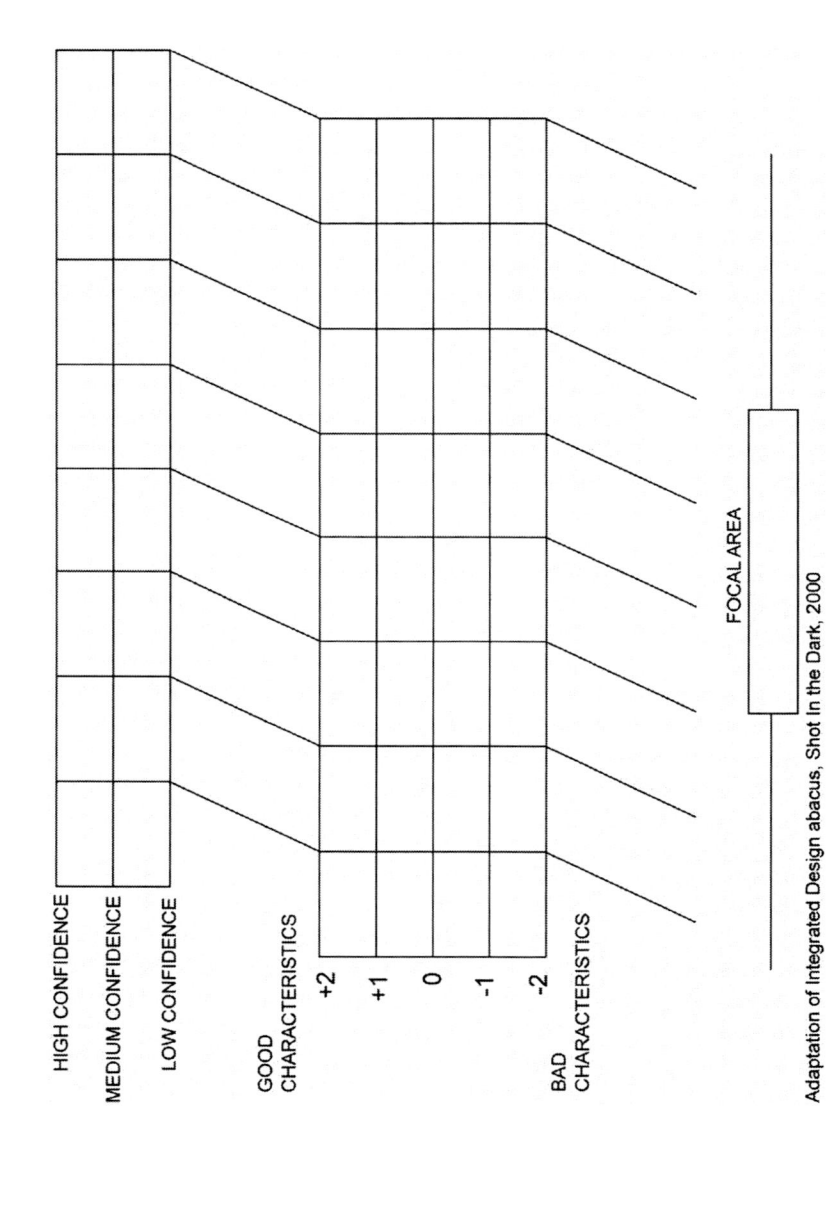

Figure 5.5 Adapted Design Abacus

Adaptation of Integrated Design abacus, Shot In the Dark, 2000

Reproduced with permission © Loughborough University

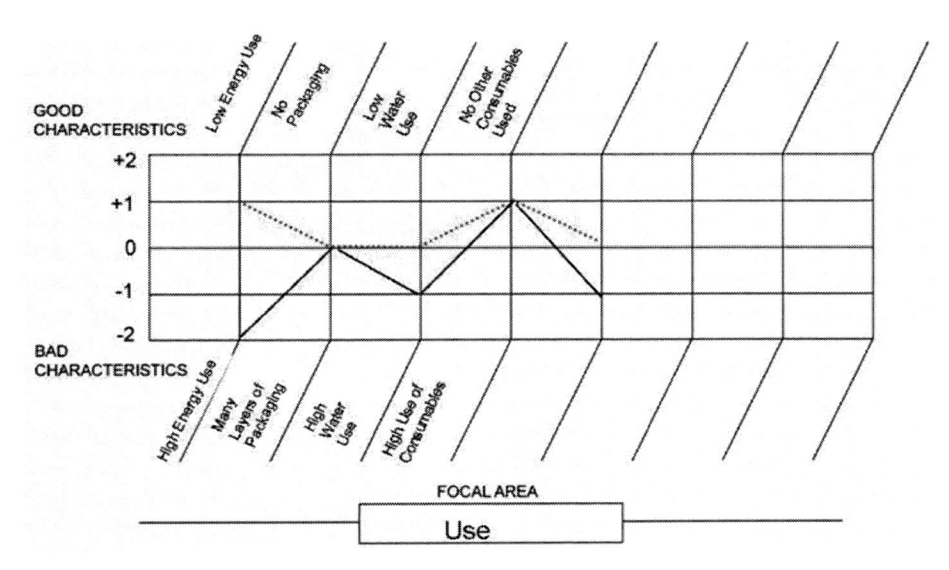

Figure 5.6 Completed Design Abacus

Reproduced with permission © Loughborough University

Using this approach, proposed products are compared with a reference product via the following five questions:

- Energy – does the proposed design use less energy than the reference product?

- Recycling – is the new product more easily recycled than the reference product?

- Hazardous waste – does the proposed product contain less chemical waste than the reference product?

- Product value – does the new design contribute to a longer product life, increase the desirability of the product and make it easier to repair?

- Service – is this a new way to provide a service with less environmental impact?

If the designers can answer YES to all of the above questions the proposed new product is an excellent alternative. If they answer 'yes' to three of the questions, the product is considered to be an interesting alternative, but one which still requires some improvement. A single 'yes' means that the designer ought instead to consider upgrades to the reference product.

SIX RULES OF THUMB

Six rules of thumb is a quick tool which helps designers focus on environmental improvements either as a brainstorming activity or to guide product development. It has emerged out of the original three Rs of reduce, reuse, recycle which have long been associated with the environment:

1. Re-think: Rethink the product and its functions.
2. Re-duce: Reduce the energy consumption and resource consumption in the whole life cycle.
3. Re-place: Replace hazardous substances with more environmentally sound alternatives.
4. Re-cycle: Use those materials which can be reused or recycled.
5. Re-use: Design in such a way that the product or parts of it can be reused.
6. Re-pair: Design a product that is easy to repair.

Idea Generation

Idea generation techniques are wide ranging and varied and can be used at any stage of the product development process. This section introduces two tools – 'Information/Inspiration' and 'Flowmaker' which have been specifically developed to help designers who are working on environmentally and socially responsible projects. It then introduces a range of general creativity techniques which can also be used to generate ideas for design for sustainability projects.

'INFORMATION/INSPIRATION'

'Information/Inspiration' (Lofthouse, 2001b) is a web based ecodesign resource for design teams interested in ecodesign. It combines inspiring ecodesign case study examples which demonstrate who is doing what in the field of ecodesign, and product focused ecodesign information which designers can apply directly to their own work, www.informationinspiration.org.uk (see Figure 5.7).

The product examples are organised in nine categories: electrical and electronic, white goods, packaging, textiles, alternative energy, furniture, concepts, green design and recycled materials. They are presented in a visual contents page that contains an illustrative icon and title for each section. Clicking on each of the images takes the user to an enlarged image of the product and a brief description of the product and its function. Case studies presented in

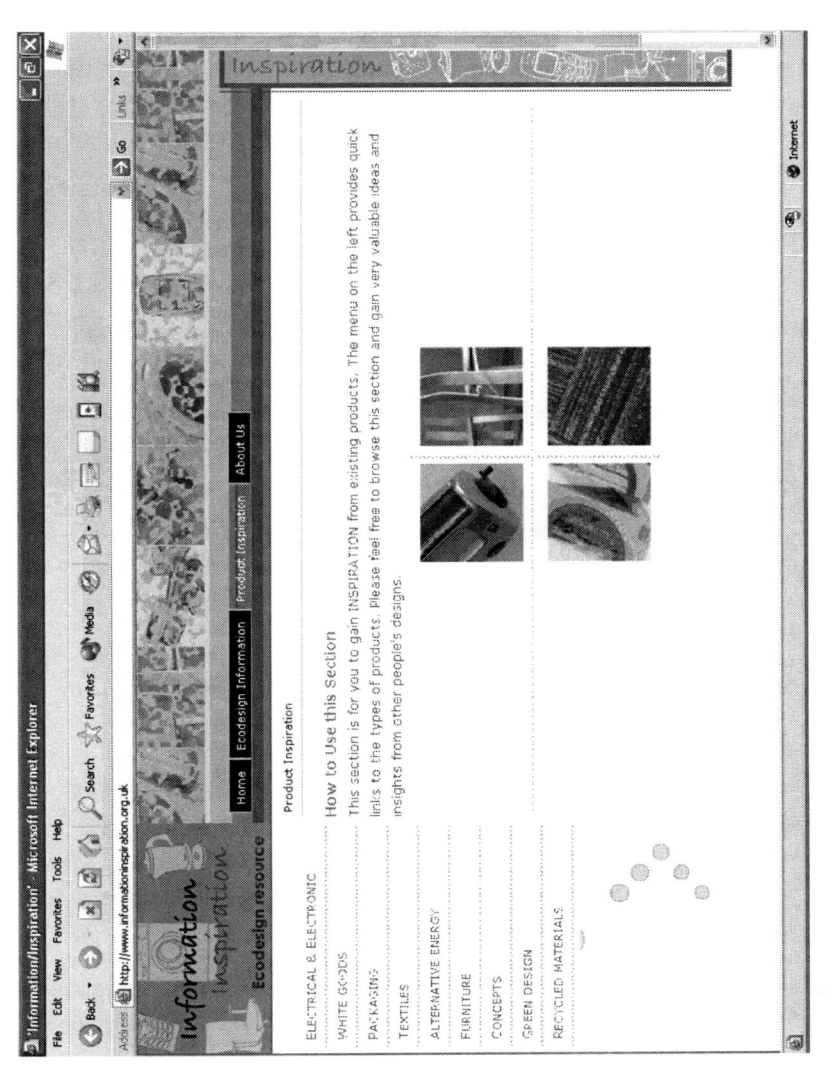

Figure 5.7 Selected page from 'Information/Inspiration'
Reproduced with permission © Loughborough University

'Information/Inspiration' include: The EcoBottle™, Conservus Fridge Freezer, Intelligent clothes pegs, Hot Shower and the Sunrise Solar Table.

Ecodesign case studies have proven to be a useful way of demonstrating that motivated companies are already successfully thinking about ecodesign. They help to provide interested designers with the inspiration and motivation to generate exciting ideas of their own. They also help to demonstrate that there is no mysterious formula to developing environmentally and socially responsible products – it is simply good design which takes into account environmental and social issues (Lofthouse, 2004).

FLOWMAKER

Flowmaker is an inspirational tool for designers, created by the WeMake design studio – www.wemake.co.uk. It takes the form of a pack of 54 cards, broken into 5 suits: Instinct, Personality, Ageing Play and Potential.

- **Instinct** explores 'design to fulfil needs' by focusing on nine related issues: feed, fight, flight, nest, philosophise, sex, social – family, social – friends, social – partner.

- **Personality** explores 'design for others' by focusing on six different pairs of personality types: active – receptive, daring – cautious, language – numbers, solo player – team player, specialist – generalist, traditionalist – futurist.

- **Ageing** explores 'design for our future selves', considering how we can make mass-manufactured products and public projects easier to use by designing to include those who are less able, but we can also look at making things harder to use, offering up challenges that promote exercise to maintain healthy function into later life. These cards encourage designers to focus on: eyesight, fine motor, flexibility, gross motor, hearing, learning, memory, smell / taste, speed and strength.

- **Play** explores 'design for joy and interaction'. Encouraging designers to design interactions that absorb us and elevate our emotions can lead to more engaging, enjoyable user experiences and help promote mental, social and physical fitness. The cards encourage reflection on: chance, copying, discovery, head spin, head to head and self-expression.

- **Potential** explores 'design for sustainability'. These cards encourage designers to make the most of the people involved, and the context in which the project sits in order to extend the material and experiential possibilities in this and future lives of the design. They encourage reflection on the following approaches: adapt, customise, cycle, dematerialise, empower, locate, maximise, meaning, mend, self-make, upgrade.

The Flowmaker cards can be used in a variety of different ways to enhance the design process, for example:

1. Random brief – Pick-up one of each colour to set out a scenario to design for.
2. Defining briefs – Select cards to reflect, probe or tighten a brief.
3. User profile – Select cards to define a user profile, to design for or market to.
4. Random word – Pick a card at random to help when a brainstorm stalls.
5. Group brainstorms – Share with colleagues, deal cards to encourage participants to look at an issue from a different angle.
6. Evaluating projects – Check against the cards suit by suit to analyse an existing design.
7. Make up your own rules.

Flowmaker aims to stimulate and inspire designers of all levels. It is an open-ended, multipurpose tool which can be adapted to support and extend design processes. It is an invaluable tool at all stages of design – to stimulate, inform, remind, nudge, jog, probe, challenge and inspire. Looking at personality type polarities helps us to put our own inclinations to one side and acknowledge different mental attitudes and behaviours. Understanding what motivates and putting the users' needs at the centre of a design process helps make a design relevant and easy to integrate into a user's life. The open format and limited content of the cards helps to stimulate the creativity of the user by supplying just enough information to get them started. Flowmaker has been used as a tool to help shape and inspire creativity sessions with corporate clients and in educational settings.

CREATIVITY TECHNIQUES

Creativity techniques are an effective way of generating new ideas for ecodesign projects and for helping you to think about a problem differently. Although it is possible to do these sorts of activities on your own they do work best in a group, as this allows you to build on each other's ideas and generate new ways

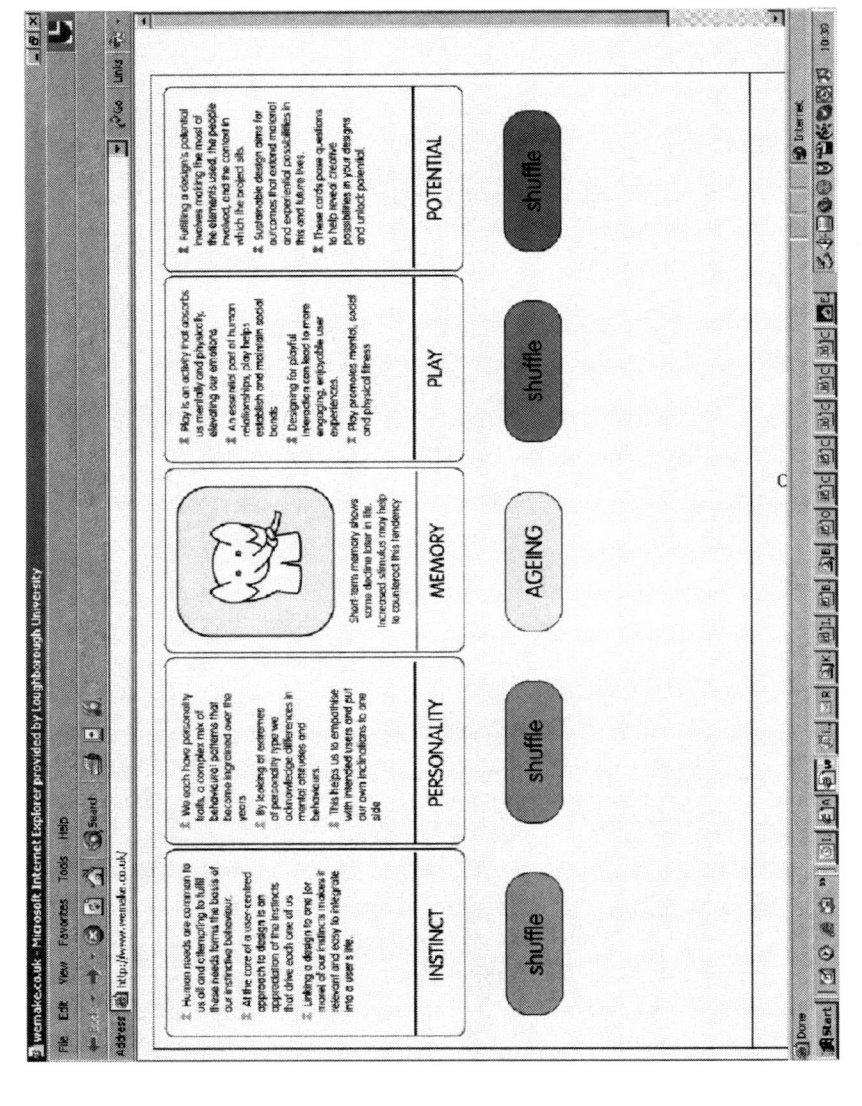

Figure 5.8 Categories covered by the Flowmaker cards
Reproduced with permission © WEmake

of thinking – which is an important element of successful ecodesign. There are also a number of rules that you have to obey: do not criticise; allow yourself to make crazy suggestions; listen to each other; and have fun. Four simple but effective techniques are listed below.

Random words can be used to help generate inspiration for problem solving and encourage you to think in different ways. To apply the technique to an ecodesign problem, select an ecodesign strategy that you want to develop ideas, for example, dematerialisation, and write this at the top of a large sheet of paper. Select a random word from a box of pre-prepared words and write the word in the middle of a piece of paper. Take three minutes to generate and record as many words associated with the random word as possible. For example, the word 'pencil' might lead to the generation of words such as 'sharp', 'point', 'wood', 'lead', 'write', 'letters', 'books', 'blue & white', 'blunt', 'rubber' and 'erase'. Once the list has been generated, apply any of the words to the challenge of dematerialisation, and record your ideas. By the end of the session a whole range of ideas related to dematerialisation will have been generated. Circle the best ideas for taking forward.

'What if?' is a creativity technique that is useful for idea generation. It helps to generate 'fresh ideas' and provide a new perspective on a problem. Again, to apply the technique to an ecodesign problem, select an ecodesign strategy that you want to focus on such as energy reduction. Generate as many 'What if…' questions as possible, related to the improvement option that you are considering: for example if looking at energy reduction you might ask; 'What if… we wanted to do the opposite?' ; 'What if… money was no object?' ; 'What if… we needed the solution tomorrow?'; 'What if… there was no oil left in the world?' Write the 'What if…' questions on the large sheet of paper, coming up with possible solutions to their questions, for example 'What if there was no oil left?' – 'We could use alternative technology like solar or wind, or we could walk/ride a bike'.

By the end of the session you will have generated a whole range of new ways of considering energy reduction. Circle the best ideas for taking forward.

Forced Relationships is a creativity technique which works by forcing the brain to jump across different repositories of knowledge. It is a challenging activity but one of the most powerful ways to develop new insights and new solutions. It is best to work in groups and to have large sheets of paper and a clear time slot available at the start of the activity. It is also advisable to have in mind a product or service that you would like to try and improve from an

Figure 5.9 Creativity session

Reproduced with permission © Loughborough University

environmental or social perspective – agree this and record it on a separate sheet of paper.

As a group imagine the Sustainable Children's Hospital of the future (2050). Talk about how it will function, what will it look like, who will work there, how do people get there, how will medicines be delivered and disposed of. Record all your ideas by writing them or drawing them on a large sheet of paper. After 10 minutes stop the activity.

The aim now is to try and force some of the ideas that you have generated into solving the problem that you agreed to investigate at the beginning of the activity. Again draw up your ideas on the large sheet of paper.

Finally switch to analytical mode. During this stage the aim is to try and determine which of the range of ideas that have been generated are the most feasible. The Feasibility Assessment table in Table 5.4 is a useful mechanism for analysing ideas. The best ideas can be listed down the left hand side and then each idea can be graded accordingly as positive/possible (+), no relation/neutral (o), negative/impossible(-) or as requiring further research (R). From this you will be able to see which of the creative ideas are the most feasible to follow up.

Backcasting is a technique that helps people create a clear vision of a preferred future; and then to devise strategies to make the preferred future happen. The outcome of back casting is a timeline with specific events and quantifiable goals needed to make the vision a reality. This technique is used by The Natural Step and is best used with a group.

To undertake backcasting participants first need to be led through a visioning exercise to develop a robust image of the group's preferred future. A vision is an image of an ideal future, one you would most like to see happen. Now the group must answer the question, 'How did it happen'? To do this, the group drafts an outline with their vision at one endpoint and today at the other. Then the group brainstorms specific events and measurable goals, which have to happen to make the vision a reality. The timeline serves as a bridge between the preferred future and the present.

Use a large piece paper for the timeline. It will be an important element of the group memory. The clearer and more specific each point on the timeline is, the easier it will be to flesh out strategies and goals. Encourage clear and specific timeline entries.

The following pieces of information must be on the timeline.

- A list of specific events (linked to present trends) that need to take place to create the vision.
- A list of milestones and goals that were achieved to reach the vision.
- The timeline must stop with the vision and begin in the present.

Table 5.4   Feasibility assessment

	Creative Ideas	Technical Feasibility	Financial Feasibility	Market Opportunities	Sustainability Feasibility	Notes
1						
2						
3						
4						
5						
6						

The questions below can be used to provoke thought and to move the process forward.

1. Have teams list the stakeholders for their vision: all the people that would have a stake in, or be affected by the changes it would create.
2. List who profits, who loses?
3. Who would be critical to making it happen?
4. Who might be able to stop it?
5. Who are all the people that need to be brought on board, consulted and involved in the implementation of this strategy?

After the timeline has been drafted, the next part of the backcasting process is to identify strategies that will lead to the events on the timeline and achieve the goals. Think Big!

You must include the specific actions and resources you think each strategy will require being successful – being as specific as possible. Be creative: use your imagination; think about what it would really take to make some of these changes happen. Next, list the stakeholders for each strategy: all the people you think would have a vested interest in or be affected by the strategy and the changes it would create.

The following questions can be useful at this stage:

1. What would a win for stakeholders look like?
2. Who profits?
3. Who loses?
4. Who would be critical to making it happen?
5. Who could stop it?
6. Who are all the people that need to be brought on board, consulted, involved in implementing the strategy?

For each stakeholder listed, briefly state what you think a 'win' on this issue would look like for him or her. What would it take to make them happy to be involved in supporting your strategy? Decide who will champion each strategy, list next steps and make it happen (Nattrass and Altomore, 2001).

User Centred Design

User centred design techniques are useful for gaining information about 'actual' user practices, habits, behaviours or needs to inform the design of a product, service or system. Techniques of this nature can reduce the potential for poorly designed or misused products; provide an insight into the complex relationship between people and their products, and record diversity of use actions. This insight helps designers better understand how people use and misuse products, which can in turn reduce the impact of product use. The following sections provide a brief description of a range of techniques available to designers, and their associated benefits and drawbacks.

PARTICIPANT OBSERVATION

Used predominately in the early stages of a project, participant observation, encompasses a range of techniques and tools designed to enable researchers to access consumers thoughts, beliefs and behaviours when using a product or service (May, 2001).

Using this technique, observation may be manual, though the use of note-taking observers located within the test environment or behind one-way mirrors (May, 2001), or via video and sound recording. There are pros and cons to both approaches. Manual observation involves manually recording verbatim, behaviours or actions in real-time. It is a demanding task which requires observers to accurately and objectively record seemingly mundane situations (May, 2001). The researcher's own interpretation of events may also influence how an action is recorded and subsequently analysed. It is also possible that differences in language use may be 'lost in translation'. On the positive side manual observation provides instant 'quick and dirty' data from which initial conclusions can be drawn (Maguire, 2001). To improve the accuracy, accessibility and quality of the approach, the researcher should write their notes up as soon as possible after the event; maintain continuity through a key words based filing system; and use different quotation marks to code paraphrased versus verbatim text to ensure accuracy when attributing comments (May, 2001). Video recording provides a comprehensive record which can be analysed at leisure, reproduced and shown to participants (Maguire, 2001). In addition video filming enables detailed footage of user actions, that is close-ups of subjects hands to be captured (Vermeeren, 1999). It also effectively captures sequential actions and allows a more general view to be taken. On the negative side, however, every hour of footage takes up to 3 hours to analyse and all verbatim must be time-logged against the video tape, coded and then grouped in appropriate clusters (Evans et al., 2002).

Using this approach, one study identified discrepancies between the way that some users use an oven and the way that it was designed to be used. While observing participants baking a cake, observations showed that they would often choose to open the oven door, to check the status of their baking rather than simply looking at it through the glass door, because they want to physically touch or skewer the cake to assess how it was progressing (see Figure 5.10). Opening the door, allows heat to escape, which reduces the overall energy efficiency of the appliance. Interestingly, the only reason that ovens have a glass door, is to allow users to visually inspect the progress of the cooking and it is actually an attribute which reduces the efficiency of the appliance (Lofthouse, 1999). Though this finding suggests that the glass panel may not be required for visual inspection, to remove it might be perceived as a regression in styling, suggesting that the window has another function in terms of style.

Figure 5.10 Participant observation exercise

Reproduced with permission © Loughborough University

USER TRIALS

User trials are simulations of product usage, in which subjects are asked to fulfil specified tasks in an experimental setting, using a product or product simulation, as shown by the examples in Figure 5.11 (Vermeeren, 1999). User trials are often undertaken as part of initial research to evaluate existing products, although they can be used to test working prototypes. Typically between eight and twenty-five users are recruited for user trials, during which they are provided with a series of tasks such as 'remove the lid from the jam jar'. Trials are ideally conducted in the customer's real environment (Maguire, 2001) and subjects are given a set time scale in which to complete the tasks. Following completion of the exercise users are interviewed about any problems or difficulties they encountered or observed. The insights gained from these interviews can enable designers to make changes which improve function, control and ease of use.

User trials provide information on user patterns and habits and allow subjects to demonstrate how they use products/services which helps to highlight ingrained behaviours and habits. They can be expensive to set up and it can be difficult to source the correct types of participants. Trials may also be affected by the type of tasks set. It is important that tasks are realistic and the way in which the task is introduced should be considered carefully. The scope of tasks and the order of tasks can also have an impact on the results. For example, knowledge gained in early simple tasks can affect the way in which the latter tasks are performed (Vermeeren, 1999). To preempt these problems

Figure 5.11 Example of user trials in progress

Reproduced with permission © Loughborough University

it is advisable to run a pilot study before the main trial. Unless observation of the effects of cumulative learning is a specific aim of the study it may be advisable to change the pilot group periodically to avoid over familiarity with the product, process or scenario. In addition, when selecting participants it may be prudent to ascertain if they have prior knowledge or experience in using a similar product.

PRODUCT-IN-USE

Product-in-use records what people actually do, not what they say they do, capturing behaviours which people may not report when asked, such as habitual behaviour. It can highlight design limitations, opportunities for improved functionality and gaps between the intentioned use of a product and actual user behaviour.

A key requirement of running a product-in-use activity is to define the scope of the research. Once identified, a research team ideally consisting of two members drawn from dissimilar backgrounds then plans the observations of the context to be studied. This may involve 'setting up a hidden camera, seeking permission to spend a day with a customer or finding suitable public locations to film' (Evans et al., 2002). The research team will then capture as much customer behaviour as possible using video or still cameras, backed up by note taking to highlight points of interest. If filming overtly, subjects must be approached and the purpose to the research explained. If filming covertly, legal advice should be sought and the recommendations put in place (Evans et

Figure 5.12 Hidden camera observations to demonstrate how users behave whilst using mobile phones

Reproduced with permission© Loughborough University

al., 2002). The image in Figure 5.12 is from a project which sought to investigate the social implications of using a mobile phone in public spaces. In this case the lady in the picture was seen to be weaving around as she speaks to a friend on the phone. Understanding how people *actually* use products helps designers to design around these behaviours.

The drawbacks of this type of technique are far reaching; they include the logistics of identifying an appropriate location and recruiting observers; the cost of and access to recording and editing facilities; and the time required to record, analyse, edit and log the data captured (May, 2001; Evans et al., 2002). However, the visual nature of the data collected has proven to be very useful for designers. It can provide stimulus for idea generation; novel adaptations by users to improve functionality may be adopted within revised product designs; and insights into 'the emotional and social context of product use' (Evans et al., 2002), misuse or alternative use of products may inspire new innovations.

SCENARIO-OF-USE

Scenario-of-use uses scenarios, props and costumes to assist in 'character building' and furniture arrangement to represent the product environment. Its key aim is to uncover previously unvoiced needs using role play as a cue for recall (Evans et al., 2002). Prior to the activity a situation of interest is identified and a basic storyline such as a 'day-in-the-life' of is generated. This is deliberately left basic and may form the first part of the workshop. The facilitators take the most important jobs in the role plays and as such must be experienced and confident. Between 5 and 20 customers are invited to attend a workshop during which they are encouraged to comment on the activities being carried out by the actors. Both the customers and the facilitator are encouraged to interrupt the action to ask questions at any point during the activity. Throughout the activity it is crucial that an informal atmosphere is maintained. Verbatim is captured and displayed along the timeline of the story. The event can also be captured on video for analysis later.

Scenario-of-use has a number of drawbacks: participants may find the activities uncomfortable if they are unaccustomed to acting; they can be time consuming and expensive to run as they require the preparation of props, costumes and furniture; and again the data can take a huge amount of time to analyse. However, scenario-of-use provides the opportunity to access previously unvoiced needs and desires that are not provided by traditional market research. Experience suggests that participants feel that they can say what they want because they are 'acting' and the process allows for relationship building between designers and customers, through increased empathy and idea generation (Evans et al., 2002). The final benefit is that customer verbatim is very difficult to ignore and proves to be a powerful tool for communicating wants and needs to higher management (Lofthouse, Bhamra and Burrow, 2005).

LAYERED GAMES

Layered games was developed during a Masters project at Cranfield University, and saw a group of students develop a series of four games to investigate insight, expectation and motivation in luxury car owners, with respect to sustainability (Holbird et al., 2003). The group sought to test the links between luxury and sustainability by embedding them within other issues or 'themes' that could be understood by the customer. This approach enabled the subject to be investigated without adversely prejudicing or leading the participants.

'Impressions' encouraged participants to consider their perceptions of themselves as luxury car owners in relation to their cars and the brand. In small groups participants were given three scales of opposing values such as 'prudent to indulgent' or 'understated to extrovert' and five cards depicting luxury cars including their own. During the activity the 'luxury car' cards were placed on the continuums by consensus, and each participant placed a card depicting their own car on each scale individually. 'Pick & Mix' sought to test participants' awareness of sustainability and the extent to which they would actively seek to reduce the environmental impact of the product. In groups of two or three, participants were asked to prioritise a series of 'luxurious' or 'sustainable' options for their cars, for example a personalised security service vs. fair trade manufacturing of parts. These options deliberately presented complex 'trade-offs' between individual benefits and local or global community well-being. In 'Money talks' (see Figure 5.13) participants were given currency in the form of stickers and the opportunity to vote for company activities that either enhanced socially responsible actions on the part of the company for example investment in improving public transport or offered luxury car owners desirable activities for example membership in an exclusive racing car club. 'Vision Map' explicitly introduced 'sustainable development' in the context of the company, customer, car and brand. Participants were asked to conceptualise their needs as luxury car owners, and how a luxury car company could adapt to support these needs in the year 2025 through engaging in a facilitated future scenario building exercise.

To enable researchers to track decision-making processes, participants were provided with individually coloured and shaped stickers, which were

Figure 5.13 Money Talks template

Reproduced with permission © Cranfield University

linked to their pre-event profile questionnaire and incorporated as 'currency' within the games. This provided a physical record of participants' journeys throughout the focus group. One of the benefits of this approach was that most of the games required the participants to record their preferences or choices manually, through placing cards on a sliding scale of attributes (in 'Impressions'), selecting and prioritising cards to depict their preference of product features (in 'Pick & Mix') using stickers as 'currency' to vote for various initiatives (in 'Money Talks') and recording the results of group brainstorming on a large scale template (in 'Vision Map'). Each game produced a tangible outcome which was collected and analysed following the event. A further benefit was that the games were simple on the surface yet concealed complex information. This allowed the researchers to draw out emotional and moral responses to scenarios, while the participants were able to enjoy the interactive and relaxed nature of the 'games'. Preparation for this type of method is key; templates must be generated prior to the event and it is often useful to display posters outlining the timing, aims and rules of each game. A potential drawback of these games is the time it takes to design and test them and, to be beneficial, they must be specifically tailored to explore a particular issue or problem.

MOOD BOARDS

Mood boards (McDonagh et al., 2002) are a collection of images selected and assembled in response to a brief. They can be generated by designers or customers to represent feelings, emotions and experiences about tasks or situations; and perceptions of product use or lifestyles (McDonagh et al., 2002; Costa et al., 2003). During the activity participants are provided with source material (brochures, magazines, newspapers, etc) scissors, glue and paper. Participants can either be given access to a range of magazines from which to select images freely, or be required to choose from a pre-selected set of images. The former approach reduces any potential bias towards pre-selected images but can be time-consuming as participants have a greater degree of decision-making to carry out the task. For the latter approach between 80 and 100 images should be provided in identical sets to avoid potential bias (McDonagh et al., 2002). The positive aspect of this approach is that it reduces the time required for participants to assemble their boards. Following image selection, participants are asked to organise the cuttings in a 'meaningful' collage (Costa et al., 2003). Two forms of analysis are typically employed; participants are invited to provide a brief explanation of the reasons for choosing each image (through notes written beside the selected images and verbally) and collages are interpreted by the researcher who typically analyses the content by searching for irregularities, commonalities and patterns such as recurring themes and issues, emerging from the collated collages (Costa et al., 2003).

Mood boards have a number of recognised benefits. They enable participants to express emotions, feelings and experiences related to products which they

Figure 5.14 Mood boards reflecting differing visions of femininity

Reproduced with permission © Loughborough University

may otherwise find difficult to express (McDonagh, Bruseberg and Haslam, 2002; Costa et al., 2003). The approach also creates tangible outcomes that designers can use as visual aids to support the ideation process (Bruseberg and McDonagh-Philp, 2001). They are also relatively inexpensive to organise. There are, however, a number of drawbacks associated with using mood boards. First of all the procedure relies on subjective interpretation. If collages are interpreted by a researcher there is a possibility of contamination of thoughts (by researcher and participants) and misunderstanding in terms of the meaning/significance of images. Secondly, as there is no prescribed formulae for mood boards, the methodological approach is open to questioning and processes must be noted and explained (McDonagh et al., 2002). Other more minor drawbacks include the time and effort the activity takes to set up, the fact that images used may be too literal (for example representing specific brands) and that users may resist taking part due to unfamiliarity.

Information Provision

'INFORMATION/INSPIRATION'

The 'Information/Inspiration' tool mentioned earlier in this chapter (www.informationinspiration.org.uk) also provides design focused ecodesign information especially aimed at the needs of designers. The information is grouped around nine key areas to make accessibility as easy as possible. Through the site designers can access a summary of different design for sustainability strategies; access and download ecodesign tools; investigate new ways of doing things; and search for information on materials, distribution and the impact of the use stage. They can also access information on end of life requirements and latest legislation requirements for designers.

REAL PEOPLE

RealPeople is a DVD based design resource that was developed at Loughborough University. It aims to make designers more aware of the specific characteristics of products that give pleasure to the people who own them. The resource contains information from an interview survey of 582 people concerning their attitudes towards functionality, usability, product pleasure and product preference as well as the results of in-depth interviews with an additional 100 people talking about their lifestyle, preferences for brands and style in general, and then describing three products that they own that give them the most pleasure. These descriptions are presented as 2-3 minute video clips, together with a breakdown of key issues. Each video clip is highly immersive, thought

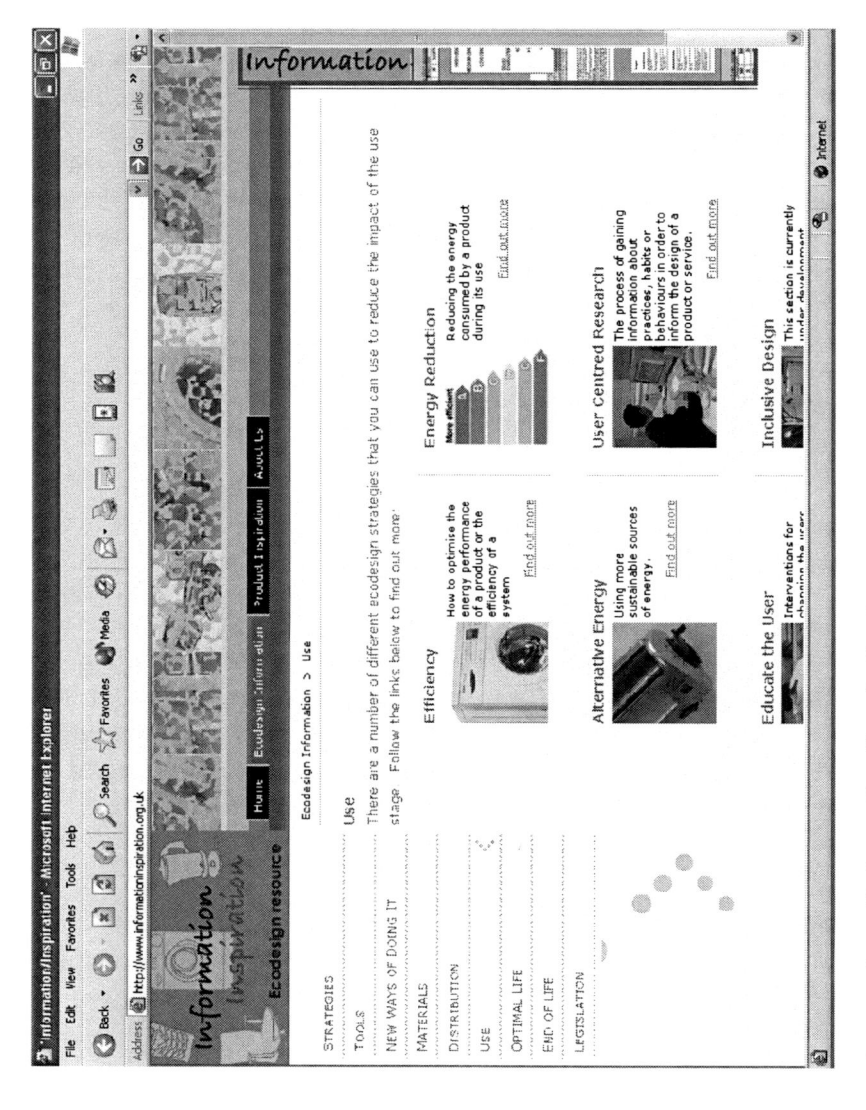

Figure 5.15 Sample page from 'Information/Inspiration'

Reproduced with permission © Loughborough University

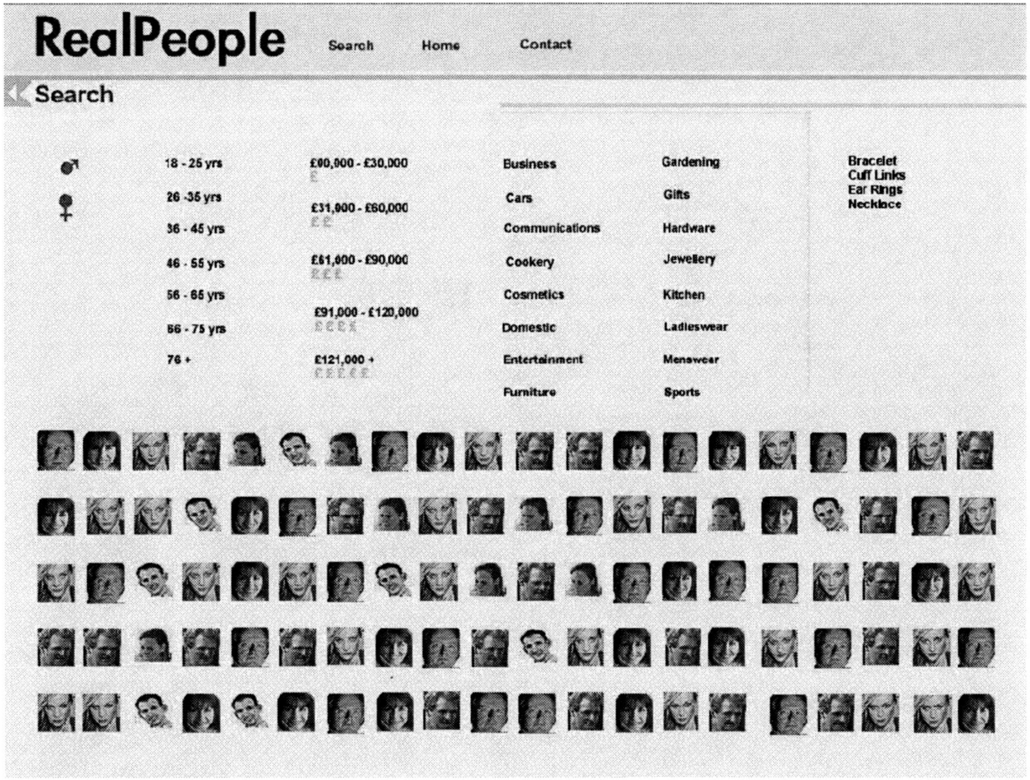

Figure 15.16 Real People search page of selection categories and people

Reproduced with permission © Loughborough University

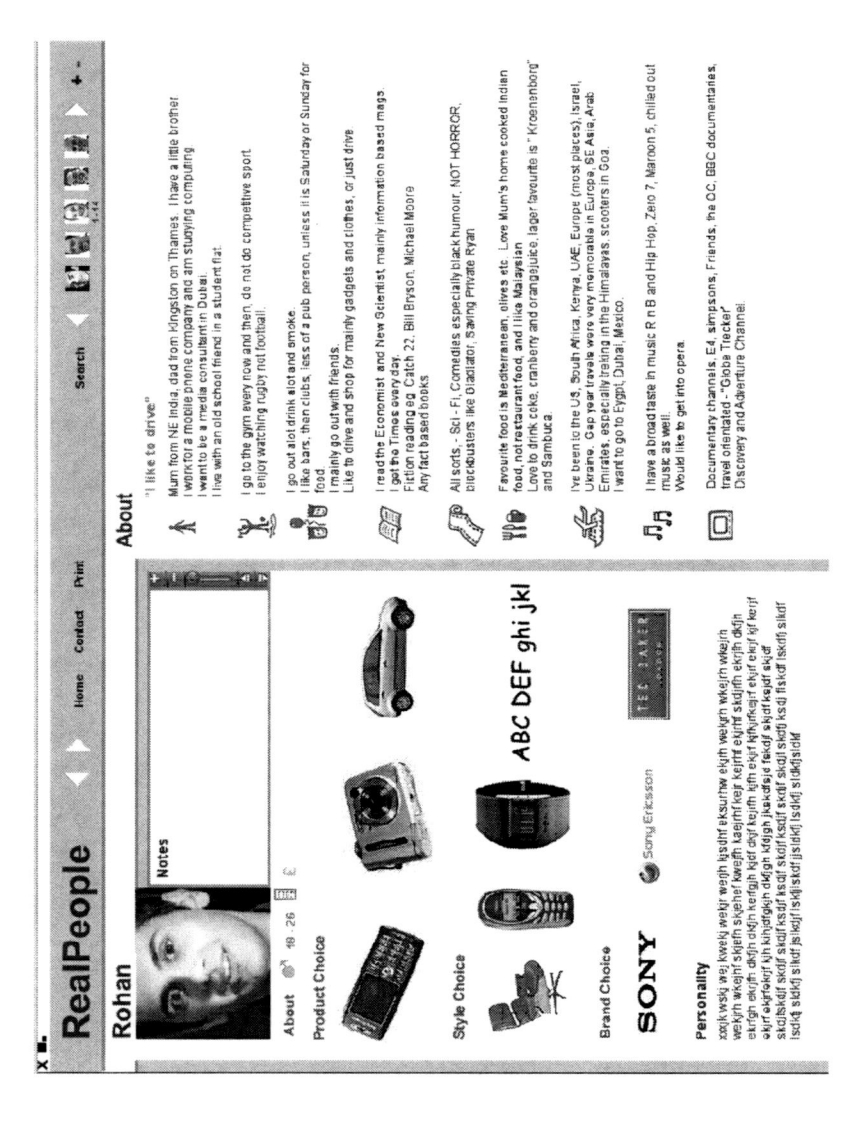

Figure 5.17 Sample page from Real People
Reproduced with permission © Loughborough University

provoking, and selected to encourage empathy between the designer and each individual in the database (Porter et al., 2005). The resource is currently being beta-tested by practising designers.

Conclusions

This chapter has introduced a range of different types of tools that can be used to support design for sustainability at every stage of the product development process. Though a quick web search will illustrate that many more tools exist, the authors believe that the selection presented here is specifically relevant to the needs of designers. Research has shown that designers need a combination of information, inspiration, education and guidance to help facilitate their involvement in design for sustainability (Lofthouse, 2001a). Combining new product-focused information with case examples gives information meaning and adds credibility to the examples (Lofthouse, 2001a). Combining information provision and education ensures that the designers have the opportunity to build up an understanding of the main principles of design for sustainability, that they can then apply to their design projects (Lofthouse, 2001a). These tools can be combined with each other and used on a pick and mix basis – to achieve a more sustainable design.

Further Information

A wide range of other tools are also available and can be sourced via the following:

Evans, S., Burns, A. and Barrett, R. (2002), *Empathic Design Tutor*, V. A. Lofthouse (ed.) (Cranfield: IERC, Cranfield University).

Mycoted Ltd (2004), *Creativity Techniques*. Available at: www.mycoted.com/creativity/techniques/index.php (Salisbury: Mycoted Ltd.).

Tischner, U. (2001), 'Tools for Ecodesign and Sustainable Product Design' In *Sustainable Solutions – Developing Products and Services for the Future*, M. Charter and U. Tischner (eds.), pp. 263–281 (Salisbury: Mycoted Ltd.).

References

Ayres, R. U. (1995), 'Life Cycle Analysis: A Critique', *Resources Conservation and Recycling*, 14:3-4, pp. 199–223. [DOI: 10.1016/0921-3449%2895%2900017-D].

Brezet, H. and van Hemel, C. (1997), *Ecodesign: a Promising Approach to Sustainable Production and Consumption* (Paris: Rathenau Institute, TU Delft & UNEP).

Bruseberg, A. and McDonagh-Philp, D. (2001), 'New Product Development by Eliciting User Experience and Aspirations', *International Journal of Computer Studies*, 55, pp. 435–452. [DOI: 10.1006/ijhc.2001.0479].

Costa, A. I. A., Schoolmeester, D., Dekker, M. and Jongen, W. M. F. (2003), 'Exploring the Use of Consumer Collages in Product Design', *Trends in Food Science and Technology*, 14, pp. 17–31. [DOI: 10.1016/S0924-2244%2802%2900242-X].

Environmental Change Unit (1997), *2MtC – DECADE: Domestic Equipment and Carbon Dioxide Emissions* (Oxford: Oxford University).

Evans, S., Burns, A. and Barrett, R. (2002) *Empathic Design Tutor*, IERC (Cranfield: Cranfield University).

Hocking, M. B. (1991), 'Relative Merits of Polystyrene Foam and Paper in Hot Drinks Cups: Implications for Packaging', *Environment Management*, 15:6, pp. 731–47.

Holbird, S., Lilley, D., Lourenço, F., Macchi, F., Gimenez, J. A. M., Stewart, K. and Wood, G. (2003), 'Integrating Sustainability into Luxury Brands of ****** and ********'*Manufacturing Sustainability and Design* (Cranfield: Cranfield University).

Lofthouse, V. A. (1999), *A Summary of Observations Arising from Ecodesign Research at Electrolux: A Report for Environmental Affairs* (Cranfield: Cranfield University).

Lofthouse, V. A. (2001a), *Facilitating Ecodesign in an Industrial Design Context: An Exploratory Study In Enterprise Integration* (Cranfield: Cranfield University).

Lofthouse, V. A. (2001b), *Information/Inspiration* (Cranfield: Cranfield University). Available at: www.informationinspiration.org.uk.

Lofthouse, V. A. (2004), 'Investigation into the Role of Core Industrial Designers in Ecodesign Projects', *Design Studies*, 25, pp. 215–227. [DOI: 10.1016/j.destud.2003.10.007].

Lofthouse, V. A., Bhamra, T. A. and Burrow, T. (2005), 'A New Way of Understanding the Customer, for Fibre Manufacturers', *International Journal of Clothing Science and Technology*, 17, pp. 349–360(12). [DOI: 10.1108/09556220510616200].

Maguire, M. (2001), 'Methods to Support Human-Centred Design', *International Journal of Computer Studies*, 55, pp. 587–634. [DOI: 10.1006/ijhc.2001.0503].

May, T. (2001), *Social Research: Issues, Methods and Process* (Buckingham: Open University Press).

McDonagh, D., Bruseberg, A. and Haslam, C. (2002), 'Visual Product Evaluation: Exploring Users' Emotional Relationships with Products', *Applied Ergonomics*, 33, pp. 231–240. [DOI: 10.1016/S0003-6870%2802%2900008-X].

Nattrass, B. and Altomore, M. (2001), *The Natural Step for Business: Wealth Ecology and the Evolutionary Corporation* (Canada: New Society Publishing).

Nokia (2005), 'Lifecycle Studies: Strategic Assessment'. Available at: www.nokia.co.uk/nokia/0,,27313,00.html

Philips Corporate Design (1996), *Guidelines for Ecological Design – Green Pages*, (Eindhoven: Philips).

Porter, C. S., Chhibber, S., Porter, J. M. and Healey, L. (2005), 'RealPeople: Designing Pleasurable Products' presented at Accessible Design in the Digital World Conference 2005, Dundee, UK.

Vermeeren, A. P. O. S. (1999), 'Designing Scenarios and Tasks for User Trials of Home Electronic Devices', in *Human Factors in Product Design: Current Practice and Future Trends*, Green, W. S. and Jordan, P. W. (eds.), pp. 47–55.

Case Studies of Product Improvement and Redesign

CHAPTER **6**

Since the 1990s applying ecodesign principles to design and development has become more widespread as companies recognise the benefits of producing environmentally responsible products, and designers become more equipped with the skills to take these issues into consideration during the design process. This chapter introduces nine industrial case studies from product, furniture and packaging design, which demonstrate how small changes to products can result in improved environmental performance.

Washing Machine, Miele GmbH

Miele GmbH is a German manufacturer of high quality domestic appliances, commercial equipment and fitted kitchens who have a strong record on sustainability. In a study by the Laundry Research Institute, Krefeld, Germany (Miele, 2006), Miele products were identified as having the longest working life in households, the average lifetime of their washing machines being 18.5 years. Miele have utilised several eco-design strategies when designing their range of washing machines, in particular, optimal service life, design for durability, design for upgradeability, reduced energy consumption and minimised resource use.

When designing for optimal service life Miele ensure that their washing machines are able to do 5,000 wash cycles (which is equivalent to an average of 5 cycles a week for 15–20 years) while maintaining the same service quality.

Design for durability is manifested through a number of features including:

- An enamel casing, which does not chip, flake or scratch easily, ensuring the appearance of the product does not diminish over time.
- A robust drum axle.

Figure 6.1   Miele washing machine
Reproduced with permission © Miele

- An unbreakable cast iron cradle which stabilises the machine and is more durable than a concrete block.

- A chrome porthole door and metal door catch designed to be opened and shut 60,000 times.

- Electronic controls which means no moving parts so less wear and tear.

All Miele washing machines are designed to be upgraded by a service engineer using a PC to allow machines to be reprogrammed in line with future updates and new programmes. This ensures that the user will want to keep their product for longer. Their machines are also designed for reduced energy consumption, attaining an AAA energy rating on top range models.

In order to minimise resource use their washing machines have self-activating ball valves, which saves detergent. During the wash cycle the floating ball presses itself tightly against the outlet of the suds container to prevent the detergent from escaping into the sump. This ensures that the expected wash performance is achieved and users do not use more detergent than is necessary. The detergent remains in the suds container, so that less is used and the environment has to cope with less pollution. The machines uses minimal water by having a drum fitted with ribs containing fins that scoop up the water and carry it to the top of the machine, which allows the product to use only 49 litres per wash.

Another feature of Miele machines is that they try to educate the user. The washing machine has a unique load size indicator that measures the size of the wash load and indicates what proportion of the manufacturer's recommended dose of detergent you should use. Finally at the end of the washing machine's life it can be recycled, and to facilitate this all casings are clearly marked by material type.

For more information on Miele washing machines visit: www.miele.co.uk

Single Use Camera, Kodak Limited

Kodak first introduced their single use camera in 1987. It was an instant hit with customers providing the first 'disposable' camera that didn't matter if it got lost or was ruined. Due to pressure from environmental groups, Kodak set about redesigning the camera to facilitate the recycling and reuse of its parts. The camera is now designed to be collected and disassembled. The resulting parts and materials are then reused or recycled, with many of them being fed back into Kodak's own manufacturing process.

Kodak cameras (see Figure 6.2) are collected at photo development booths and returned to one of three collection facilities. All packaging, front, back covers and any batteries are removed. The plastic casing is passed through a metal detector to check for traces of metal, then shipped to be reground into flake and reused in cameras or other products. All discarded paper packaging is sent to a recycling centre. The removed batteries are tested, and if they meet certain quality standards then they are used:

- internally for employee's pagers,
- donated to organisations as 'gifts-in-kind' or
- sold as recycled batteries.

The camera frame, metering system and flash circuit board are rigorously tested and fed back into the manufacturing system for re-use. The cameras are cleaned in an ionised-air vacuum system then visually inspected on a manual assembly line. Old viewfinders and lenses are replaced with new ones – for quality purposes. Many small parts such as the thumb wheels (for advancing film) and counter wheels (for counting the number of exposures left) are reused. Finally the subassemblies are sent to one of Kodak's three single use

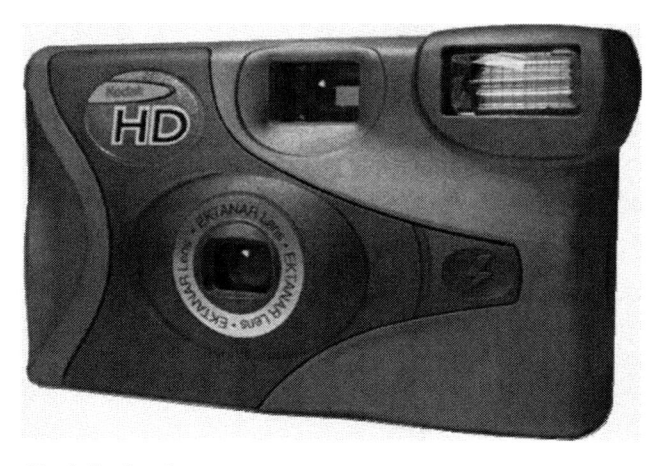

Figure 6.2   Kodak single use camera
Reproduced with permission © Loughborough University

manufacturing plants for assembly as a new product, where fresh film, new battery and outer packaging (35 per cent recycled post-consumer waste), and additional packaging is added (Kodak, 2001; Lewis et al., 2001, Kodak Environmental Services, 2002).

Ecobottle, Sarda Acque Minerali S.p.A

Designed and manufactured in Italy by Sarda Acque Minerali S.p.A., the Eco Bottle is a 1.5 litre plastic bottle made totally from polyethylene terephthalate (PET). In the past traditional drinks bottles have been made from a PET body, and separate cap made from one of a number of materials including HDPE and LDPE and in many cases additional materials such as paper, inks and adhesives for the labelling. The main drivers for this have been a combination of ensuring a secure closure between the top and the bottle (coefficient of friction) and ensuring that the legal information requirements are met on the labels of bottles containing food. This combination of materials has made bottle recycling difficult and time consuming.

The manufacturers of the EcoBottle have designed around these constraints and created a bottle, screw top and seal which are 100 per cent PET, with no label, no glue, no paper, no ink and no paint (see Figure 6.3). PET is commonly used to package soft drinks and water, and is popular because it is inexpensive, lightweight, resealable, shatter-resistant and recyclable. It is also chosen for its strength, thermo-stability and transparency (NAPCOR, 2004). The design of the Ecobottle is based on one of the simplest ecodesign principles of using a single material in the design, but has lead to great advantages. The result is a light water bottle which is easily returnable and can be recycled without any particular treatments.

All the required information can be embossed directly on the bottle by a laser machine or created through deformation of the mould tools. It is the first bottle with Braille characters embossed. A seal sleeve on the screw top allows application of the bar code and of colours that identify the company.

After the water has been consumed and the bottle is no longer needed, a purpose-made tool, given free with the bottle can be used to cut the bottle in half. Nothing is thrown away and even the screw top stays screwed to the bottle (Sarda Acque Minerali SpA, 2004). Once they have been cut in half the parts can be stacked together, the lower half twists exactly inside the upper part, the first bottle is the container for all the following bottles. The low neck means that the height of the stack only increases by 2 cm for each bottle added. No other bottle can be stacked with the Ecobottle which helps keep the materials gathered pure PET. Once the column has reached 1 m it can be taken to the nearest collection point for recycling.

As the collected material is pure PET, it does not need to be manually or mechanically separated. A simple grinding and washing procedure is all that is required to obtain PET-flour. Recycled PET can be used to make many new products, including fibre for polyester carpet; fabric for T-shirts, underwear,

Figure 6.3 Close up of the Ecobottle

Reproduced with permission © Sarda Acque Minerali SpA.

athletic shoes, luggage, upholstery and sweaters; fibrefill for sleeping bags and winter coats; industrial strapping, sheet and film; automotive parts, such as luggage racks, headliners, fuse boxes, bumpers, grilles and door panels; and new PET containers for both food and non-food products (NAPCOR, 2004).

For more information visit the company website at http://ecobottle.com or http://san-giorgio.com

Azur Precise Irons, Royal Philips Electronics K.V

Royal Philips Electronics K.V, based in the Netherlands, have an established track record for considering sustainability in the design of their products. The top ecodesigned products at Philips achieve Green Flagship status. This means that after having gone through divisional ecodesign procedures, a product or product family has been investigated in three or more of the Green Focal Areas and proven to offer better environmental performance in two or more of those areas. The Philips Green Focal Areas are weight, hazardous substances, energy consumption, recycling and disposal, packaging and lifetime (for lighting). The Azur iron (see Figure 6.4) is one of the Green Flagship products.

The Azur Precise 4330 has been benchmarked against both the best commercial competitor and other commercial competitors, with a focus on packaging, weight and recyclability.

Figure 6.4 Azur Precise Iron

Reproduced with permission © Philips International BV

Designed for maximum comfort, efficiency and safety, the iron's ergonomic features include knobs and a handle that provide maximum comfort and ease of use. Compared with the average of its three closest competitors, the Azur Precise weighs 5 per cent less and the environmental impact of packaging is 50 per cent less. Philips is on a par with all competitors on recyclability.

Medisure Monitored Dosing System, The Boots Company

The Boots Company, in the UK, have a programme to review, and where possible improve the sustainability of their packaging systems. In the case of the Medisure system it was recognised that there was potential for the PVC content to be replaced and for the gauge thickness to be reduced. The suggestion originated as a consequence of the Quality and Buying Departments working together.

The monitored dosing system for medicinal tablets is a service offered to nursing homes and care institutes by 340 Boots stores in the UK. The idea was to replace existing 0.025 mm PVC with 0.0175 mm APET in blisters. These are heat-sealed in-store against an aluminium foil. Due to the large number of blisters used by patients *per annum* there were significant benefits to be made by reducing the overall packaging. This has led to savings of 34.5 tonnes of material *per annum*.

Boots designed and amended the new pack format making it easier for customers to use. The cavities in the blisters were made marginally deeper and wider to accommodate a wider range of tablets that were previously causing a problem with some of the operators. The new pack had improved features,

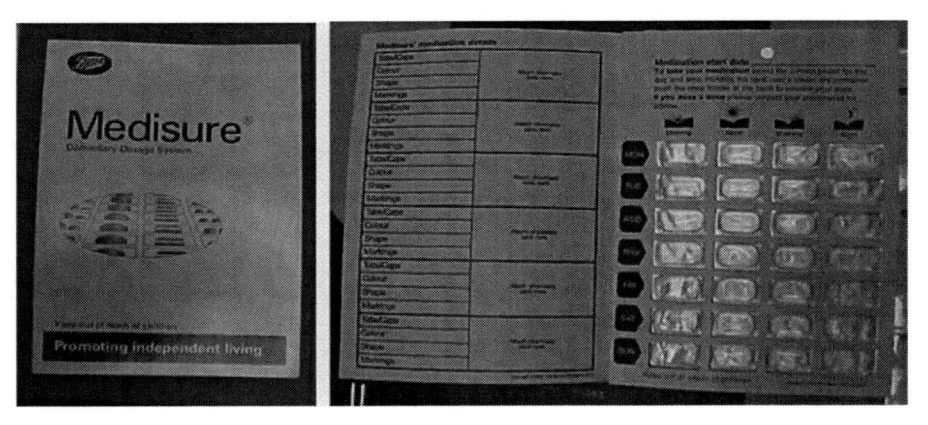

Figure 6.5 Medisure packaging

Reproduced with permission © Alliance Boots

in addition to improved traceability (date of manufacture, cavity numbering, and so on).

The empty blisters are now thinner so more can fit in the same size outer packaging to reduce relative transport costs. The final product has an APET blister sealed to an aluminium foil so cannot be recycled after use.

Life Chair, Formway

Working in collaboration with RMIT in Melbourne, Australia, Formway applied ecodesign principles to the design of their LIFE Chair (see Figure 6.6).

The design team aimed to avoid the use of problematic materials such as PVC. The foam used for the seat and arms is blown without chlorofluorocarbons (CFCs) that are known to damage the ozone layer. The medium used to manufacture the foam is water.

Recycled materials were used for the metal components wherever possible. The total recycled content of the chair is 52 per cent by weight. The highest recycled content is 100 per cent for some of the aluminium components, up to 90 per cent for some zinc components and up to 20 per cent for ABS, nylon and acetal. At this stage some of the nylon components cannot incorporate

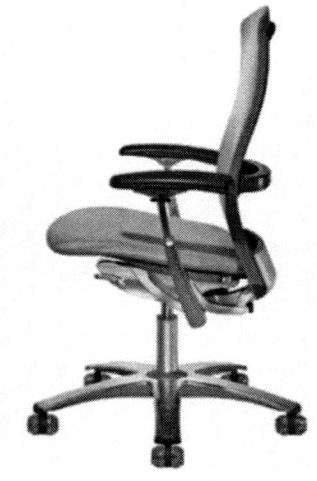

Figure 6.6   Formway LIFE Chair

Reproduced with permission © Formway

recycled content due to a loss of properties in the recycling process, however, opportunities to switch to recycled nylon are still being evaluated.

Processes that are known to have a higher impact on the environment, such as powder coating of metal components, were avoided. The elimination of powder coating not only reduces overall material consumption, it also avoids the generation of solid and hazardous waste by-products, especially the liquid wastes and processes required to pre-treat powder-coated components.

Wherever possible production scrap is reprocessed in-house, for example post-industrial plastic scrap from the injection moulding process is granulated and fed back into the injection-moulding machine. All aluminium scrap is recycled.

The use of adhesives for the assembly process was avoided wherever possible to make the disassembly process easier, and to minimise emission of volatile organic compounds (VOCs) in the workplace. VOCs are emitted from adhesives, paints and some plastics, and research has linked emissions to poor indoor air quality and 'sick building syndrome'. Productivity losses of up to 6 per cent have been identified among staff working in buildings where indoor air quality is poor and is estimated to cost companies billions of dollars annually in lost productivity (CSIRO Manufacturing and Infrastructure Technology, 2005). The LIFE chair has replaced most of the adhesives with alternative fastening mechanisms such as snap fits, hinge pins or spring clips.

Another highly significant feature of the LIFE chair is the improved ergonomics, which will contribute to a healthier workplace and more productive workers.

The LIFE chair weighs only 15 kg, which is significantly lighter than competitive products that weigh between 18 and 25 kg. LIFE also has fewer components – only 177 compared with over 200 for one competitor. Such a reduction translates into approximately 18 per cent fewer components than its primary competitor. This facilitates easier disassembly, reuse and refurbishment, as well as materials recycling when LIFE reaches end-of-life. One obvious example of the light-weighting strategy is the back of the chair, which is made from a knitted fabric with an optional plastic lumber support. The knitted fabric has replaced the conventional plastic back with foam and upholstery fabric.

The LIFE chair has been designed for durability – LIFE provides a 10 year warranty compared with the more common 5 year warranty. Increased durability has been achieved through Finite Element Analysis and Design Validation tests specifically aimed at eliminating weak points and maximising product longevity. The lack of any damage-prone finishes such as powder coating also reduces aesthetic deterioration and the risk of premature obsolescence, disposal and waste.

The LIFE chair has been designed for reuse and refurbishment. Many of the components, including the seat and back sub-assemblies, seat, back and arm toppers, the aluminium base and the upholstery are easy to remove, replace or retrofit. It has been designed for disassembly to assist in repair and refurbishment as well as recycling:

- Elimination of most adhesives apart from soft tops and labels – these have been replaced with snap fits, hinge pins or spring clips which are easier to take apart.

- A reduction in the total number of components.

- Seat and back toppers do not need tools to be assembled or disassembled.

- Only a screwdriver, Allen key, mallet and pair of pliers are needed to dismantle the whole assembly.

- A reduction in the number of components will facilitate easier reuse, refurbishment and recycling. In this regard LIFE outperforms similar chairs currently in the marketplace. LIFE has approximately 18 per cent fewer components than its primary competitors.

- The LIFE chair incorporates other features that improve recyclability. Most of the plastic parts have in-mould labels to help identify the different plastics so that they can be separated for recycling. The labels are from the international standard for labelling.

- Most of the materials used in manufacturing the chair are technically recyclable (for example aluminium, steel, ABS, polypropylene, nylon and polyurethane foam).

While a large percentage of the chair is technically recyclable, a system would obviously need to be put in place to collect, disassemble and recycle them. Formway and its partners are currently investigating the possibility of establishing a take back scheme in certain markets. Collectively, the Ecodesign features embodied in LIFE directly and indirectly contribute to improved waste avoidance, waste reduction, reuse and refurbishment, as well as materials recycling when LIFE eventually reaches end-of-life.

For more information visit Formway's website at www.formway.co.nz/flash.html or the RMIT website at www.cfd.rmit.edu.au

Furniture Transport Packaging, Segis SpA

Segis SpA in Italy consider the whole life cycle of the furniture they produce. Specifically they consider: material used, durability of materials, care of items during transportation, volume and the end of the product's life. One of their first initiatives was to manufacture the seats and backs of a number of their models from recycled plastic content. More recently they were approached by a customer in North East Europe, 900 km away from their factory, to produce and deliver about 40,000 pieces of furniture per year. This inspired another initiative, to consider how they could reduce the environmental impact and costs of manufacturing these products, while still maintaining a high level of customer care and product quality.

Using the traditional transportation system of four chairs per carton would have meant 150 boxes of 600 chairs per truck. For an average of 40,000 pieces per year, this would have meant producing 10,000 boxes which would then have to be transported to their end destination 900 km away, by 70 full trucks a year. All of this would have been expensive and used a great deal of resources, in terms of materials and fuel. In response to this problem Segis redesigned their delivery system.

They produced a series of trestles into which they could stack between 20 and 30 chairs (depending on whether the model had armrests or not) without boxes and protection (see Figure 6.7). As a result every truck can now take between 1,000 and 1,100 products rather than the 600 products which were transported previously. This rethink eliminated the need to manufacture, pay for and transport the boxes, and the number of trucks needed to transport the chairs was reduced by nearly 50 per cent. This resulted in a total reduction of labour and costs of over 15 per cent on the total cost of the item, as well as considerable savings on pollution and material consumption. The extra costs of the process included the initial investment into the trestle production and a truck journey every 8 weeks to collect the empty trestles on the return trip. This system has been in place for nearly 5 years and Segis have produced and transported nearly 250,000 products.

Figure 6.7 Segis SpA transportation systems

Reproduced with permission © Segis SpA

When Segis were approached by a large North American furniture producer they adapted the trestle and made similar savings in the container shipment. The low cost trestles can be returned or used further in their country. Segis are now in their second year of collaboration and have shipped 30,000 pieces of furniture to the US.

Sustainable Brush Manufacturer, Charles Bentley & Sons

Charles Bentley & Sons, a UK-based manufacturer of wooden sweeping brushes, have developed a holistic approach to the management of the materials sources that they rely on while reaping additional social and environmental benefits. Through careful management they make sure that value is added at every stage of the life cycle of the rubber trees that they source their material from.

The sweeping brushes sold at hardware and DIY retail outlets are manufactured from rubber trees which grow in Sri Lanka, India and Asia. The trees are farmed for rubber by the local people for 25 years until they can no longer be tapped for rubber. During this time beehives are put into the plantations to enable local people to manufacture honey.

At the end of the tree's life it is cut down and the tree trunk is used to provide the raw material for the brush heads. The branches of the tree are processed locally into charcoal which can be sold locally for fuel and horticultural purposes. The root balls of the rubber trees are sold to farmers in Japan for the production of Shitake mushrooms. The rubber tree wood is then shipped to the UK for manufacturing.

During the manufacturing process wooden shavings are generated when the brush head is machined and the hole for the handle is created. Bentley recognised another market opportunity for these waste shavings and the potential for selling them as animal bedding, under the Bentley brand. Wedge shape offcuts from rough cut timber are used by the Navy to plug up leaks which appear below the water line of the metal hulls of their boats. The small pieces of wood which can be wedged into the cracks then expand (due to the water) to fill the gap.

By taking a creative view of the whole product life cycle Bentley have generated a number of social and environmental benefits. They have generated jobs for the local communities in Sri Lanka, India and Asia through the production of honey, and utilising the whole tree through good forest management of the plantations and forest areas. They meet the standards of the

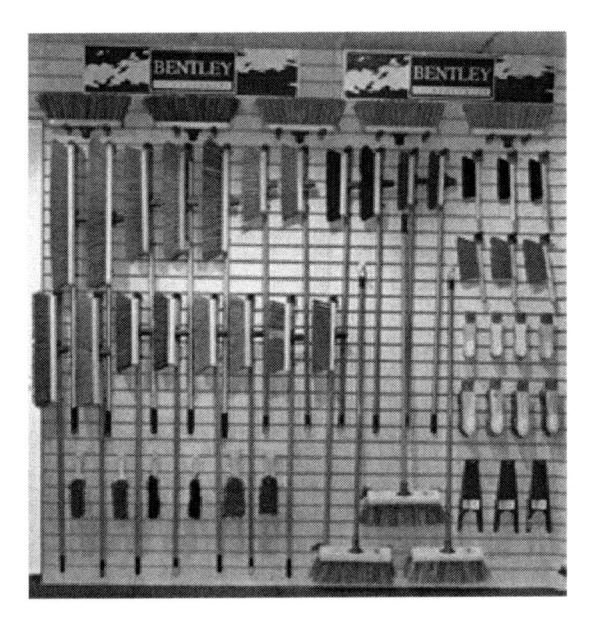

Figure 6.8 Product range offered by Charles Bentley & Sons Ltd.

Reproduced with permission © Charles Bentley & Sons Ltd.

Programme for the Endorsement of Forest Certification, the leading certification standard and the only one of its type to have the full backing of the United Nations Forestry Forum. They have achieved environmental benefits through sustainable farming, reducing waste and using resources carefully. Finally they have reaped economic benefits by selling the by-products which would have previously been waste.

iU22 Ultrasound Machine, Royal Philips Electronics K.V

The Medical Systems division at Philips was an early adopter of ecodesign finding it to be a specific customer requirement. In light of this the Philips iU22 ultrasound system combines intelligent design, a wide range of high-performance features and significant environmental improvements (see Figure 6.9). Built using a modular approach the iU22 system meets the stringent requirements necessary to be named a Philips Green Flagship product. Compared with its predecessor, the iU22 weighs 22 per cent less, eliminates 82 per cent of the hazardous substance mercury, reduces energy by 37 per cent, uses 20 per cent less packaging and offers a 30 per cent improvement in total weight of recyclable material.

In addition to its environmental attributes, the iU22 system's features include next generation, real-time 4D imaging, voice-activated control and annotation, and automated image optimisation technologies. The iU22 system responds to a raising demand for diagnostic imaging services and increased cost restraints. In one ultrasound system, clinicians get superb image quality, improved examination efficiency, greater automation and advanced ease of use.

An independent study found that the iU22 system provides the best overall ergonomic accommodation for facilitating neutral working postures, which reduces biomechanical stress in the neck and shoulders – the most common musculoskeletal injury suffered by sonographers and sonologists. It was also found to be the only system among six comparable systems that met the industry recommendations for independent height adjustment of the monitor and control panel and for the full range of viewing distances.

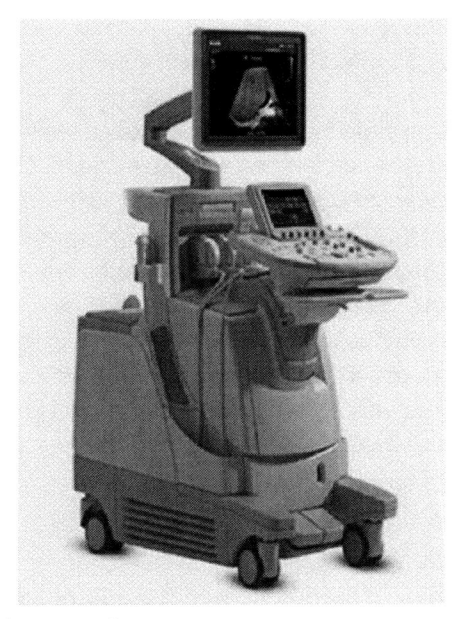

Figure 6.9 iU22 ultrasound system

Reproduced with permission © Philips International BV

Mobile Phones, Nokia

The Finnish company Nokia are the world's largest manufacturer of mobile phones. Nokia have made a specific commitment to reduce the environmental impact of their products across the entire life cycle, as part of their corporate society responsibility agenda (Nokia, 2004). They have identified a range of priority areas:

- Energy efficiency of the products.
- Knowledge of product material content.
- Considerations concerning the quantity and type of materials used in the product.
- Promoting efficient use, reuse and recycling of materials through product design (Nokia, 2004).

Mobile phones currently have a very high throughput in the market. They contain high levels of valuable metals. Nokia are involved in research into design for disassembly methods to identify the most cost-effective ways of disassembling their phones to retrieve these materials. Currently, 65–80 per cent of the material content of a mobile phone can be recycled and reused (Nokia,

2006). Nokia mobile phones are shredded, sorted into different materials streams and recyclable or valuable materials extracted.

The Nokia 5510 prototype has smart materials integrated into its design to facilitate active disassembly at the end of the product's life (see Chapter 4 for more details). The active components remain dormant until triggered and are designed so that they cannot be triggered during normal use of the product. However, at the end of the product's life the collected phones are heated to a predetermined temperature and the shape memory alloy actuators curve to open the snap fits holding the cover, display and display window in place (see Figure 6.10). In addition to this the shape memory polymers used to manufacturer the screws and screw bosses open to release their screws, which lose their threading (Tanskanen, 2003).

Conclusions

This chapter has outlined how designers can begin to address environmental issues in the development of products. The case studies outlined represent only a small proportion of the mainstream products which are now on the market from companies such as Philips, AEG, Electrolux, Huntleigh Healthcare, Herman Miller, Bang and Olufsen, Hewlett Packard, Apple, Russell Hobbs, Miele, Patagonia, Baygen, Wilkhahn, and Blueline to name but a few. They provide a powerful demonstration of the progress that has been made in this

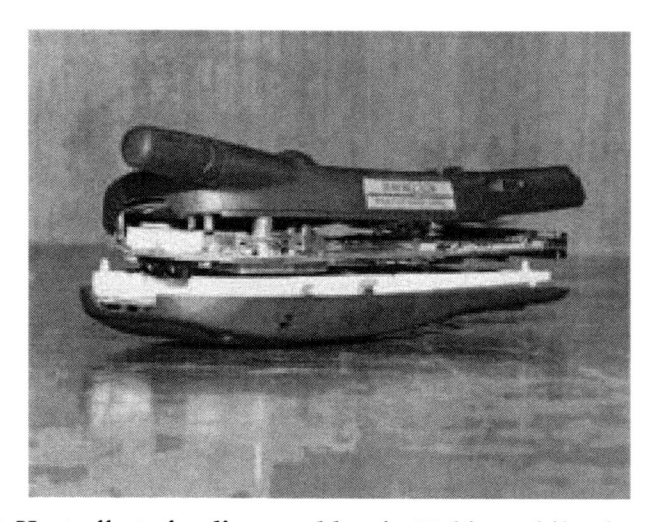

Figure 6.10 Heat effects for disassembly of a Nokia mobile phone

Reproduced with permission © Dr. Joseph Chiodo, Active Disassembly Research Ltd.

arena and illustrate how a life cycle approach can lead to effective incremental improvements, and innovative and competitive products for manufacturers.

Chapter 8 will take design further and introduce case studies which are not only environmentally responsible but also adopt a system or service approach in their move towards sustainability.

References

CSIRO Manufacturing and Infrastructure Technology (2005), 'Indoor Air Pollution – Assessment and Control' (Melbourne: CSIRO Manufacturing and Infrastructure Technology). Available at: ww.cmit.csiro.au/brochures/res/indoorair

Kodak (2001), 'A Tale of Environmental Stewardship: the Single-Use Camera'. Available at: www.kodak.com/US/en/corp/environment/performance/recycling/suc.shtml

Kodak Environmental Services (2002), 'Recycling One-Time-Use Cameras'. Available at: www.kodak.com/US/en/corp/environment/kes/recycling/otuc/usMinilabs.jhtml

Lewis, H., Gertsakis, J., Grant, T., Morelli, N. and Sweatman, A. (2001), *Design + Environment, a Global Guide to Designing Greener Goods* (Sheffield: Greenleaf Publishing).

Miele (2006), 'Washing Machines'. Available at: www.miele.co.uk

NAPCOR (2004), 'What is PET?'. Available at: www.napcor.com/whatispet.htm (Sonoma, CA: NAPCOR).

Nokia (2004), 'Environmental Report of Nokia Corporation'. Available at: www.nokia.com

Nokia (2006), 'Nokia Website'. Available at: www.nokia.com

Sarda Acque Minerali SpA (2004), 'EcoBottle – A Fast PET Recycling System'. Available at: http://ecobottle.com/home_eng.htm (Selargius: Sarda Acque Minerali SpA).

Tanskanen, P. (2003), 'A New Life for Old Electronics'. Available at: www.nokia.com/nokia/0,,5719,00.html (Nokia Research Centre).

Systems and Services – Looking to the Future

CHAPTER 7

This chapter examines how design for sustainability can use systems innovation and a service view to achieve greater sustainability improvements. It focuses on how design is set to change, with the shift away from products towards services and how designers can influence the way in which 'functionality' is delivered to consumers.

Systems Approach to Design

There is a growing movement of researchers and practitioners who are moving away from existing thinking in design for sustainability towards more of a systems approach to problem solving.

CRADLE TO CRADLE

Traditionally, design for sustainability has focused on minimising environmental damage, with the ultimate aim being to achieve zero-waste. However, McDonough and Braungart (2003) argue that the problem with this approach is that it results in destroying the environment 'a bit less' rather than stopping the destruction all together. Rather than aiming to become more efficient, they argue that we need to aim to be more effective by focusing on improving the whole system to create a situation where increased consumption leads to quicker damage reduction. If it can be achieved, this is an attractive proposition, as it provides a positive agenda for design and it supports the economy, the environment and society (McDonough and Braungart, 2003).

McDonough and Braungart (2003) propose a cradle to cradle approach to design, through which the outputs (or waste) from one system become the inputs (nutrients) for other processes or products. This approach to design ensures that the whole system is more sustainable rather than just one particular element. The basic principle of this approach is the creation of nutrients, whereby waste equals food, where everything is beneficial for the material flows.

Through the cradle to cradle approach every process and material is examined and the emissions and waste produced, are identified. The overall aim is to ensure that toxicity (to both humans and the environment) is minimised, unsuitable waste is reduced and nutrients are increased. This approach is trying to replicate the cyclic system that happens naturally within nature.

The cradle to cradle approach identifies two distinct cycles, the biological nutrient cycle and the technical nutrient cycle. This distinguishes between two types of products, products of consumption such as food where everything gets changed biologically and chemically by being used, and products of service like a television, things that are just used and don't change their state. So in order to adopt this cradle to cradle approach designers need to identify whether they are designing a technical or a biological thing and try to ensure that there is a way of completing the cycle so all nutrients are used usefully.

> **Climatex fabric**
>
> McDonough and Braungart worked with DesignTex and a Swiss textile mill, RohnerTextil AG, to create an attractive and functional fabric that could be safely returned to the environment at the end of its useful life. It was a challenge to identify materials that were functional, environmentally sound, and socially just. In the end they chose a combination of free-range wool and ramie both for their comfort and moisture wicking properties and because they were safe for the environment. The team also partnered with Swiss chemical manufacturer Ciba and EPEA, to select 38 chemical dyes, auxiliaries, and fixatives that met performance criteria and were not harmful to plants, animals, humans or ecosystems. The resulting fabric, Climatex®Lifecycle™, has gained many design awards, has proved to be tremendously successful in the marketplace, and is also so safe that its trimmings are used as mulch by local gardening clubs (Climatex, 2006).

SYSTEM INNOVATION

This idea of systems innovation and the benefits gained from design for sustainability are illustrated in Figure 7.1. The model shown identifies four distinct types of innovation linked with environmental improvements over more than a 20-year timeline (Brezet, 1997). The first type of innovation is product improvement. This is where existing products are improved with regards to pollution prevention and environmental care and products are made compliant with legislation. The second type of innovation focuses on product redesign, in this case the concept stays the same, but parts of the product are developed further or replaced by others. Typical aims here are an increased reuse of spare parts and raw materials, or minimisation of the energy used at several stages in the product life cycle, as illustrated by the case studies outlined in Chapter 6. The next level of innovation, function innovation, involves changing the way the function is fulfilled. Examples of this are provided in Chapter 8 and include a move from paper-based information exchange to email, or private cars to car share systems. The highest level of innovation focuses on system innovation in which new products and services, which require changes in the related infrastructure and within organisations, are developed. Examples of this type of innovation might include a change from traditional agriculture to industry-based food production (Brezet, 1997).

Figure 7.1 illustrates that moving from Level 1: Product improvement to Level 4: System innovation requires and achieves increased eco-efficiency, takes more time and provides a greater complexity of input. This model suggests that these more complex innovations will only be achieved over a significant time period and by organisations that begin to consider sustainability and system interactions, but that through this approach it is possible to achieve higher levels of environmental and social improvement and business benefit.

Services

People in the Western world are now living in a service economy. According to Euromonitor in 2000 68 per cent of the EU gross domestic product was generated by services (Euromonitor, 2000). In industrialised countries there has been a general economic shift from making products to providing services. Between 1950 and 1990, manufacturing declined from 35 to 20 per cent of gross

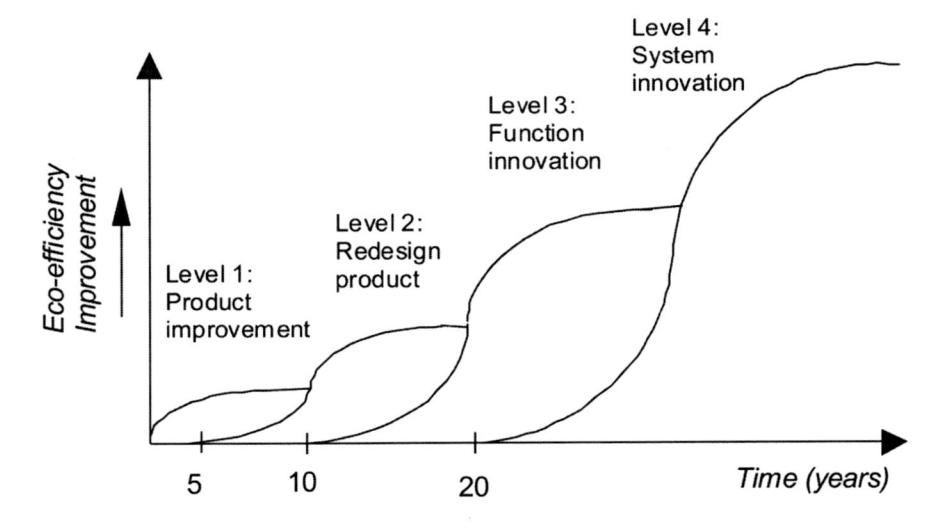

Figure 7.1 Model of ecodesign innovation (Brezet, 1997)

domestic product in the UK, while services increased from 32 to 57 per cent (Roy, 2000). This did not happen overnight. The traditional industrial economy, where value is attributed to material products which are exchanged, has shifted towards the new service economy, where value is more closely related to the performance and the real utilization of the products integrated in a system (Giarini and Stahel, 1993). Services have become indispensable in making products available that fulfil basic needs (Giarini and Stahel, 1993).

In addition, services are being increasingly embodied in the products we buy. This is reflected in the innovative effort and expertise that is captured in the final value of the products. In some cases, the rising demand for products with a higher service-orientated content is having an impact on the ways that companies perceive themselves. Many manufacturing companies now consider that service-related activities drive their business, as it is now the services that they offer rather than the product they manufacture that create the largest income stream (Seyvet, 1999).

By adding services to their products, companies can obtain a higher level of producer-customer interaction, which enables them to develop a better product service mix and increase competitive advantage. Clearly the service economy is steadily stretching its boundaries. A useful way to view this growth in services is the move from the sale of product to the sale of function or utility (White et al, 1999).

To date, the move from selling products to providing services has not been driven by environmental concerns but instead by business motives (European Commission, 2001; Goedkoop et al., 1999; Rocchi, 1997; Mont, 1999, White et al, 1999, Zaring et al., 2001). These include increasing competitiveness, reducing costs, serving a market's need for speed, providing customer convenience and flexibility, improving corporate identity, or responding to a discrete business opportunity (Rocchi, 1997; White et al, 1999). However, the concept of taking a service approach is recognised by the United Nations Environment Programme (UNEP) as a means to reduce the environmental footprint of production and consumption patterns (UNEP-DTIE, 2000; UNEP-DTIE, 2001).

FROM PRODUCTS TO SERVICES

One of the continuous themes of this book is the recognition that organisations need to significantly reduce their environmental impact. One of the ways of doing this is to look for alternative methods of delivering product function – moving from products to services. Many authors agree that a move to services can provide the opportunity for the introduction of concepts that significantly improve the environmental performance of production and consumption systems (Goedkoop et al., 1999; White et al, 1999, Brügemann, 2000). As outlined earlier, Brezet (1997) believes that adopting a service approach could lead to huge environmental improvements.

This shift in the manufacturer's role from providing products to providing services is also known as the 'functional economy', and has been linked to the creation of a more environmentally sustainable economy. This is not only one in which customers are users of function and services rather than consumers of product, but also one where the economic objective is to create the highest possible use value for the longest time while consuming as few resources as possible (Stahel, 1997).

Dematerialisation is the process of moving away from a material product to a more virtual delivery of the service. A good example of dematerialisation is the move from music stored on compact discs to downloadable virtual music. The 248 songs which can currently be stored on a 2MB MP3 Player, would have previously required about 16 CDs. This new form of delivery also creates added functionality such as increased portability, easier access and flexibility.

Types of products and services

The distinction between products and services can be difficult to define. In practice, there is a continuum of products and services, in which the total offer is a product-service mix. The mix encompasses a certain share of material, physical aspects and the remaining share of non-tangible aspects. This is represented in Figure 7.2 which illustrates five types of products and services ranging from pure products to pure services:

1. Pure tangible product – a product without an accompanying service, such as salt or soap.

2. Tangible product with accompanying services, such as a car with a guarantee.

3. Hybrid – equal parts of products and services, such as a restaurant.

4. Major service with accompanying minor products and services, such as an airline.

5. Pure service, such as babysitting.

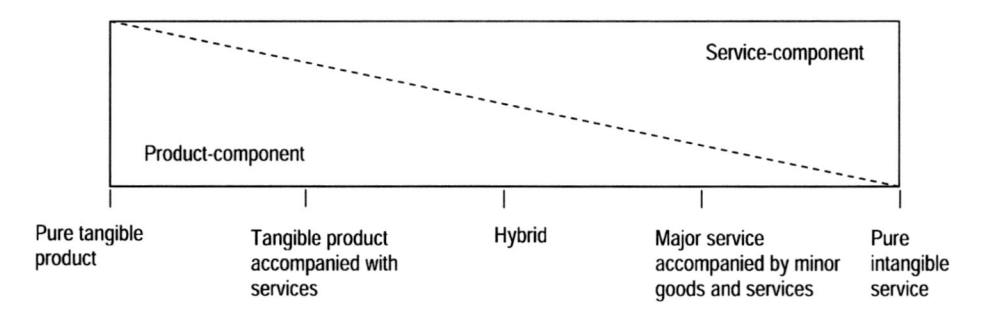

Figure 7.2 Product-service continuum (Kotler, 1994)

Pure tangible product | Tangible product accompanied with services | Hybrid | Major service accompanied by minor goods and services | Pure intangible service

Services can be viewed as the bridge between the physical entity and the customer need. Often, the main objective of a service is to provide added value to the customer in order to secure user satisfaction and gain a competitive advantage in the market place (Coskun et al., 1992). In today's market, where mobility and flexibility are of high importance, it is recognised that the customer no longer wants ownership of certain products, but rather they want the utility or function provided by products (Popov and DeSimone, 1997). Services are therefore a key method for giving the customer what they want.

Stahel (1999) outlined a comparison between the existing industrial economy where products are sold and the future service economy where performance is sold. This is illustrated in Table 7.1 and highlights advantages from both a company and consumer perspective.

The services that are of interest within the field of sustainable development are known under many different names: eco-services, eco-efficient services, sustainable services, product-service systems, sustainable service systems, and sustainable product-service systems. In this book, the term *eco-services* will be used.

TYPES OF ECO-SERVICES

Eco-services are either closely related to products or else they substitute products. They can generally be divided into three categories (Hockerts, 1999) and can be considered in the form of a 3-step matrix of: product-orientated services; use-orientated services; and need-orientated services (see Figure 7.3). These definitions all apply to services that are a substitution for products.

Table 7.1　Comparison of the service and industrial economies (Stahel, 1999)

SALE OF PERFORMANCE (service economy)	SALE OF PRODUCT (industrial economy)
Performance, customer satisfaction, results	The object of a sale is a product
Seller is liable for the quality of the performance (usefulness)	Seller is liable for manufacturing quality (defects)
Payment if and when the performance is delivered (no fun, no money)	Payments for and at transfer of the property rights (P-O-S transaction)
Work in situ (service), around the clock, no storage or exchange possible	Work centrally/globally (production), products can be stored re-sold, exchanged
No transfer of rights and liability to user	Rights and liability transferred to the buyer
User advantages: • flexibility in utilisation • cost guarantee per unit • zero risk • status value as performance	User advantages: • rights to increase in value • status symbol as product
User disadvantages: • no right to increase in value	User disadvantages: • zero flexibility in utilisation • no cost guarantee • full risk for operation and disposal
Marketing strategy – customer service	Marketing strategy – publicity, sponsoring
Notion of value – utilisation over long term period	Notion of value – high short term exchange value at point-of-sale

Product-orientated services

Product-orientated services are characterised by customer ownership of the physical good, and represent only a minimal departure from a traditional sell-buy arrangement. These services enhance the utility that ownership of the product delivers to the customer, through warranties and maintenance agreements for example (White et al, 1999). The environmental motivation for manufacturers to adopt product services is that they increase the lifetime of the product to which they are attached, for example a maintenance service for a washing machine. As a result, over time fewer machines are needed, and materials and energy are saved. Besides the environmental motivation there is an attractive business motivation as well; the experience of some manufacturing companies is that they gain a steady income from the service and help to tie

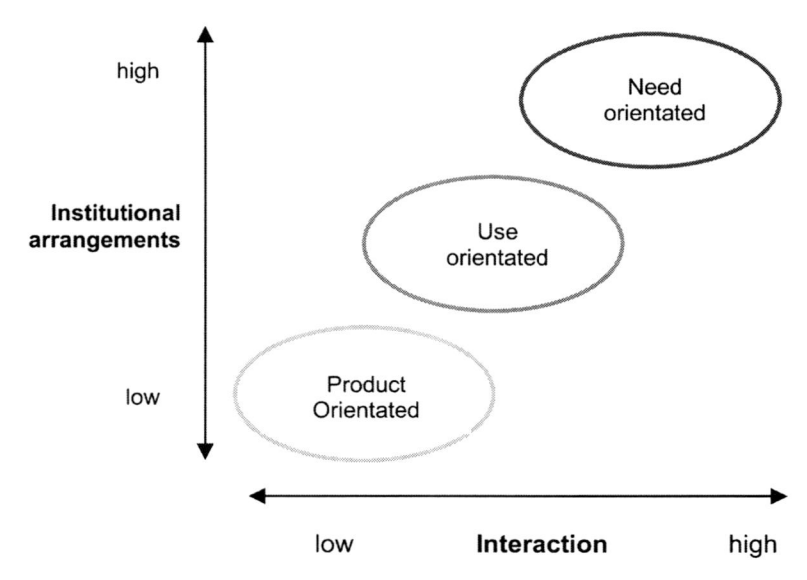

Figure 7.3 Three Service Concepts (Hockert, 1998)

the customer into the company for longer (Hockerts, 1998). In addition to this by reducing the amount of resource and energy consumption per unit of performance, these services contribute to the traditional bottom line of a company, and can lead to increases in profit.

Use-oriented services

In the case of use-orientated services, ownership of the product resides with the service provider. Customers have the use of the product, but maintenance as well as end of life disposal is the responsibility of the service provider (White

---

Xerox

Prior to 1987 Xerox produced 60 tonnes of landfill waste each year which was costing them around US$4.1 million a year. By moving to take back and equipment remanufacture, Xerox Europe saved US$80 million in costs and diverted 65,000 tonnes of material from landfill.

Xerox established a product-orientated service whereby their photocopiers were leased to companies which enabled them to be returned for upgrading, maintenance and remanufacture. They also began to offer a results-orientated service where customers paid for numbers of copies and Xerox supplied all the equipment, paper and toner in order to deliver high quality outputs.

By taking this approach to business Xerox designers have been given the opportunity to create more functions and enable more uses of their products but with fewer materials. Design now considers sustainability from initial concepts and has an ethos of 'Waste-free products form waste-free factories for waste-free offices' (Xerox, 2000).

et al, 1999). Thus, the consumer gains the function of the product without ownership, that is there is merely a temporary transfer of material goods from the provider to the customer. Traditional rental or leasing arrangements fall into this category, such as tool-rental, taxis, and car-sharing schemes. With rental systems, consumers can use products for some time without the need to purchase and to own them. The expected increased eco-efficiency rating for use services is closely related to the high use intensity of products, which brings about a reduction in the number of products needed. For example, when people share a car, fewer cars are needed to make the total amount of desired travel kilometres. Producers or providers are being paid for the units of service as delivered to the customers. They therefore have an economic interest in reducing the use of resources (materials and energy) in the production of each unit of service. In addition, all costs will be shared between all the units of service over the entire life cycle.

Results-oriented services

Finally, in the case of result-orientated services the product is owned and run by the supplier, who therefore has an incentive to intensify and optimise the product's operation, and to increase its service life. A pesticide manufacturer for example, offers farmers an 'integrated pest management' service. They train and assist farmers in the use of pesticides. They can save up to 50 per cent of pesticide costs and at the same time increase yields because many crops react adversely to an excess of pesticide. In a more developed version the pesticide provider could even offer a 'crop insurance' service, guaranteeing the customer that certain pests will not affect its yield. The whole pesticide application would be carried out by the service provider (Hockerts, 1999). As this example illustrates, how the customer's need is satisfied is irrelevant, as long as it is satisfied. An additional aspect of result services is that by developing and offering a result instead of a pre-specified product or service, the environment can be considered from the start. Consequently, significant reductions in the material and energy consumption per unit of service are envisaged (van der Zwan and Bhamra, 2001). Chemical Management Services (CMS), for example, are services where the chemical supplier manages the chemical procurement, delivery, inspection, inventory, storage, labelling and disposal of chemicals for industrial customers. By managing everything linked to chemicals, CMS firms promise use reductions to their customers, inverting the traditional supplier-customer relationship from one where profits are tied to sales to one where profits are tied to efficiency (White et al, 1999).

Summary of different types of service approaches

Three different types of service approaches have been introduced above, illustrating three different levels of complexity in terms of the company's relationship with their customer. Table 7.2 provides an illustration of how these approaches might manifest themselves for three products: a lawn mower, washing machine and car.

DRIVERS FOR ECO SERVICES

There are a range of drivers which encourage companies to offer eco services, these include the threat of legislation, responding to client's wishes, the company considering themselves environmentally and socially responsible, and the move towards green purchasing by authorities.

It is envisaged that a move from products to eco services would result in fewer waste management concerns from the domestic and manufacturing sector, a more sustainable economy based on higher levels of service, and increased employment (UNEP-DTIE, 2001). More jobs per unit of material product are created by labour-intensive services such as take back systems, repair, refurbishment, or disassembly. They also provide jobs to local markets, and thus contribute to strengthening the local economy, since services are generally closely tied to location.

For consumers the shift towards eco services would result in lower costs and fewer problems associated with the buying, use, maintenance, and eventual replacement of products (UNEP-DTIEy, 2001). The quality of the service, and consumer satisfaction, may improve with eco services because the service provider has the incentive to use and maintain equipment properly, increasing both efficiency and effectiveness. It might also result

Table 7.2   Service examples (Sherwin, 1999)

	Product-orientated perspective	Use-orientated perspective	Need orientated perspective
Lawn mower	Guarantee, maintenance, repair, take back	Sharing and pooling, Communal use.	Gardening service
Washing machine	Repair man, maintenance	Product rental, functional sales, visit to laundry	Laundry service, collection and delivery
Car	Extended warranty, regular services	Car leasing, car share, car rental	Transport, mobility, public transport, Internet

in greater diversity of choices in the market, in terms of maintenance and repair services, payment schemes, and different schemes of product use that suit the customer better in terms of ownership responsibilities (Mont, 1999).

BARRIERS TO ECO SERVICES

There are, however, considerable barriers to overcome when companies aspire to offer eco services. Most companies lack the experience to design service methods and management systems (UNEP-DTIE, 2001). Offering services requires a deeper understanding of business and production processes and a greater degree of trust is required when the service provider takes over what have previously been in-house activities (White et al, 1999). There is generally a poor understanding of costs associated with eco services (and services in general) both on the supply and demand side, making it difficult to determine how to charge for knowledge and information (White et al, 1999). There is often a lack of information available to consumers to influence their purchasing decision, relating to issues such as lifetime costs of ownership (Cooper and Evans, 2000; UNEP-DTIE, 2001). For some types of services, customer psychology can be an important barrier, since offering services can mean moving towards a situation of non-ownership, especially since current economic and social infrastructure has developed to reinforce individualistic lifestyles and routine activities based on private consumption (UNEP-DTIE, 2001; White et al, 1999; Cooper and Evans, 2000).

ENVIRONMENTAL EFFECTS OF ECO SERVICES

Although eco services have been heralded as a solution to decouple economic growth from the consumption of natural resources (Goedkoop et al., 1999) the environmental implications of introducing eco services have not really been studied in detail (Mont, 1999). There is so far no conclusive evidence that the use of these services contributes positively to sustainable development (Mont, 1999). However, the general assumption regarding the beneficial environmental effects of the eco services approach is based upon the expectation that because producers are being paid for the units of service delivered to the customers, producers get an economic incentive to optimise the amount of resources used. This economic incentive would in turn stimulate technological, organisational and marketing innovations directed towards services that are optimised over the entire life cycle, since all costs over the complete life cycle will be the responsibility of the company (Meijkamp, 2000).

Table 7.3 outlines a number of possible advantages and disadvantages of eco services (European Commission, 2001). Apart from the environmental drawbacks, a service strategy is not always preferable, as it could be rejected by product-orientated companies, may not be accepted by customers, and there could be a rebound effect (Brügemann, 2000).

The rebound effect is the negative environmental effect which can arise from providing customers with a service (Mont, 1999; Zaring et al., 2001). The more the price of something reduces, the more likely it is that demand will increase in response to this. Therefore, if eco services result in falling prices for particular activities or goods (for example, because energy or material requirements are reduced), the demand for them is likely to increase. The

Table 7.3 Possible advantages and drawbacks of renting and leasing (European Commission, 2001)

Environmental implications of renting	
Possible environmental advantages	**Possible environmental disadvantages**
• Reduction of purchased goods • Ability to use more expensive goods of a higher environmental performance (depending on the product the environmental implications might be + or -) • Improved maintenance • Intensive use of products	• Ability to use more expensive goods of a higher quality (in the case of cars this might lead to a higher use of fuel) • For specific products more transport is needed • Decrease of product responsibility • Purchase of products after trial period
Environmental implications of leasing	
Possible environmental advantages	**Possible environmental disadvantages**
• More possibilities for environmental chain management (recycling, product reuse) • Leasing facilitates monitoring of products during phase of use and upon return and disposal • Leasing company's interest in prolonging the durability of the product leased • Possibility to realise an optimal technical life span • Appliances more efficient in use • Ability to use more innovative technologies, for example solar systems and heat pumps	• Stimulation of additional demand resulting in higher material flow • Leasing products age faster than products owned by the user • Less product responsibility in case of operational lease might lead to irresponsible use • Easier replacement of products • More intense use in case of financing independent of use (for example leased cars)

question then is whether the environmental impact as a result of the increase in demand eliminates the reduced environmental impact per unit of output. Three levels of rebound effect have been identified (Zaring et al., 2001):

- Direct effects – where the introduction of a new service creates additional demand for a closely related product or activity.

- Indirect effects – where the introduction of a new service creates additional demand for linked products or activities.

- Platform effects – where new services influence the general factors determining the level and patterns of production and consumption. For example, e-learning services create better educated, richer individuals who consume and travel more.

It should be noted that some of these rebound effects would be considered positive from an economics perspective.

WHAT ECO SERVICES MEAN FOR DESIGN

Design activity is likely to change significantly if the move to eco services increases. Designers need to be able to view their role in the development of eco services clearly and not be threatened by the rise of the service economy. As outlined earlier in the chapter, eco services by their very nature will be made up of a mixture of products and service. The interesting challenge for designers is that current products are unlikely to be entirely suitable to be used as part of eco services and which presents an interesting design opportunity. It is likely that products for eco services will need to be more durable than those that exist today and may have different features which reflect the need of the service.

For designers it is important to recognise that services as compared with products are intangible and therefore often difficult to display, communicate and price. They are also heterogeneous, that is they can contain a diverse range of different components, which could make it difficult to ensure quality and customer satisfaction. Services also differ from products in that production and consumption are simultaneous rather than separate and therefore mass production (and the economies of scale that go along with it) may be difficult to achieve. Products in general are regarded as non-perishable but this may not be the case with a service as it is not possible to store a service or build stock. The supply of services must be highly synchronised with demand as they cannot be returned or resold (Zeithaml and Bitner, 1996; Gabbott and Hogg, 1997).

Conclusions

Systems and services are expected to become more prolific in the coming years. It is anticipated that these will be affected by a number of consumer and industry trends. Consumer trends include the rise of mass-customisation whereby many more products are customised to the requirements of the consumer; in addition the consumer has come to regard product and service as two parts of the same commercial deal, thus blurring the border line between product and service.

Industry trends include increasingly flexible production networks and lean organisations resulting from the fact that the consumers can decide which products are made and at which time in the durable goods sector. Services are now regularly brought in to bridge the gap between production infrastructure and individual demand. Trends in the service industry include increasing use of hard- and software to raise service level or to reduce costs.

Recent changes in environmental policy refer to the need for a combined change in production and consumption; considering systems and services can enable designers to make a significant contribution to this. Finally recent visionary documents from governments have started to announce the need for system changes to tackle sustainability in a holistic rather than a piecemeal manner. Chapter 8 provides a range of case study examples that illustrate how these principles can be applied.

References

Brezet, H. (1997), 'Dynamics in Ecodesign Practice', *UNEP IE: Industry and Environment,* 20, pp. 21–24.

Brügemann, L. (2000), 'MSc Project Exploratory Study on Eco-Efficient', Doctoral thesis (The Netherlands: T.T.U. Delft).

Climatex (2006), 'Climatex Lifecycle'. Available at: www.climatex.com

Cooper, T. and Evans, S. (2000), *Products to Services* (London: Friends of the Earth Trust).

Coskun, A., Samli, L., Jacobs, W. and Wills, J. (1992), 'What Presale and Postsale Services Do You Need to Be Competitive', *Industrial Marketing Management,* 21.

Euromonitor (2000), 'Euromonitor', p. 142 (London: Euromonitor).

European Commission (2001), *Eco-services for sustainable development in the European Community* (Brussels: European Commission).

Gabbott, M. and Hogg, G. (1997), *Contemporary Service Marketing Management* (London: Dryden Press).

Giarini, O. and Stahel, W. (1993), *The Limits to Certainty: Facing Risks in the New Service Economy* (Dordrecht, The Netherlands: Kluwer Academic Publishers).

Goedkoop, M. J., Van Halen, C. J. G., Te Riele, H. R. M. and Rommens, P. J. M. (1999), 'Product Service Systems, Ecological and Economic Basics Report of Pi!MC, Storrm C. S. & Pré Consultants', Commissioned by the Dutch Ministries of Environmental and Economical Affairs.

Hockerts, K. (1998), 'Eco-efficient Services Innovation: Increasing Business-Ecological Efficiency of Products and Services' in *Greener Marketing: A Global Perspective on Greening Marketing Practice*, Charter, M. and Polonsky, M. J. (eds.) (Sheffield: Greenleaf Publishing).

Hockerts, K. (1999), 'Innovation of Eco-Efficient Services: Increasing the Efficiency of Products and Services' in *Greener Marketing: A Global Perspective on Greening Marketing Practice*, Charter, M. and Polonsky, M. J. (eds.), pp. 95–108 (Sheffield: Greenleaf Publishing).

Kotler, P. (1994), *Marketing Management; Analysis, Planning, Implementation and Control* (Englewood Cliffs, NJ: Prentice-Hall, International Inc.).

McDonough, W. and Braungart, M. (2003), *Cradle to Cradle: Remaking the Way We Make Things* (New York: North Point Press).

Meijkamp, R. (2000), 'Changing Consumer Behaviour through Eco-Efficient Services: An Empirical Study on Car Sharing in the Netherlands', Doctoral Thesis (The Netherlands: Delft University of Technology).

Mont, O. (1999), 'Product-Service Systems, Shifting Corporate Focus from Selling Products to Selling Product-Services: A New Approach to Sustainable Development' AFR Report No.: 288 (Sweden: Swedish EPA).

Popov, F. and DeSimone, D. (1997), *Eco-Efficiency – The Business Link to Sustainable* (Cambridge, US: Development, MIT Press).

Rocchi, S. (1997), 'Towards a New Product-Services Mix: Corporations in the Perspective of Sustainability', Doctoral Thesis (Lund, Sweden: Lund University).

Roy, R. (2000), 'Sustainable Product Service Systems', *Futures*, **32**, pp. 289–299. [DOI: 10.1016/S0016-3287%2899%2900098-1].

Seyvet, J. (1999), 'Presentation at the O.E.C.D. Business and Industry' Policy Forum on Realising the Potential of the Service Economy (Paris: O.E.C.D.). Available at: www.oecd.org/dataoecd/10/33/2090561.pdf

Sherwin, C. (1999), *Service Design: from Products to Service – Satisfying Consumer Needs Using Eco-Efficient Services* (Cranfield: Cranfield University).

Stahel, W. (1997), *In the Industrial Green Game: Implications for Environmental Design and Management National* (Washington, DC: Academy Press).

Stahel, W. (1999), 'From Products to Services or Selling Performance Instead of Goods' presented at Ecodesign '99: 1st International Symposium on Environmentally Conscious Design & Inverse Manufacture IEEE Computer Society, Japan.

UNEP-DTIE (United Nations Environment Programme Division of Technology, I. a. E) (2000), 'Product Service Systems: Using an Existing Concept as a New Approach to Sustainability', provisional draft, Expert Meeting on Product Service Systems Paris, France.

UNEP-DTIE (United Nations Environment Programme Division of Technology, I. a. E) (2001), 'The Role of Product Service Systems in a Sustainable Society', Brochure, Paris, France.

van der Zwan, F. and Bhamra, T. A. (2001), 'Alternative Function Fulfilment: Incorporating Environmental Considerations into Increased Design Space' presented at 7th European Roundtable for Cleaner Production (Sweden: Lund).

White, A. L., Stoughton, M. and Feng, L. (1999), *Servicing: The Quiet Transition to Extended Producer Responsibility* (Boston: Tellus Institute).

Xerox (2000), 'Recycling Systems'. Available at: www.fujixerox.co.jp/eng/ecology/report2000/pdf/14-20.pdf

Zaring, O., Bartolomeo, M., Eder, P., Hopkinson, P., Groenewegen, P., James, P., de Jong, P., Nijhuis, L., Scholl, G., Slob, A. and Örninge, M. (2001), 'Creating Eco-Efficient Producer Services', Report 15th February 2001, Gothenberg (Gothenberg, Sweden: Research Institute).

Zeithaml, V. and Bitner, M. (1996), *Services Marketing* (Singapore: McGraw-Hill).

Case Studies of Systems and Services

CHAPTER 8

Chapter 7 demonstrated how new ways of thinking about the way that we deliver products with a system or service view can lead to greater improvements in sustainability. This chapter introduces ten case studies from a wide range of sectors which illustrate a more radical approach to product delivery and show how these approaches can result in substantial environmental improvements in combination with other benefits for the customer, company or society.

Mirra Chair, Herman Miller

Since the 1950s Herman Miller have considered themselves to be 'stewards of the environment' and have a commitment to corporate sustainability. They have a Design for the Environment (DFE) team who apply environmental design standards to both new and existing products using the McDonagh-Braungart Cradle-to-Cradle Protocol (outlined in Chapter 7). New product designs are evaluated with respect to material chemistry and safety of inputs, disassembly and recyclability (Herman Miller, 2005). The Cradle-to-Cradle approach ensures that the product is considered as part of a wider system and therefore designed to minimise environmental impact across all elements of the system.

The Mirra Chair (see Figure 8.1) was the first office product to be developed from the beginning under the guidance of the DfE team. It was successfully launched in 2003. The chair is constructed from steel, plastic, aluminium, foam and textile and as a result is 96 per cent recyclable at the end of its useful life. The chair also uses 42 per cent recycled material of which 31 per cent is post-consumer waste (Herman Miller, 2005).

Other key features of the materials selected for the chair's design include:

- Most metal components are powder coated which eliminates solvents and volatile organic compounds from the finishing process.

Figure 8.1 Mirra Chair

Reproduced with permission © Herman Miller Limited

- All plastic components have marking to aid recycling.
- No PVC is used.
- The moulded polymer used in the chair back can be recycled up to five times.
- Several textiles are available with 100 per cent recycled content.
- Packaging materials include corrugated cardboard and a polyethylene bag, which are both part of a closed loop recycling system (Herman Miller, 2005).

Herman Miller's commitment to sustainability extends to their manufacturing facility where the production line for many of their products (including the Mirra chair) utilises 100 per cent green power, 50 per cent from wind turbines and 50 per cent from captured landfill off-gassing. No air or water emissions are released during the chair's production and all solid wastes are recycled as much as possible (Herman Miller, 2005).

In terms of the product's performance key features include easy assembly for cost-efficient and quick replacement of parts, easy disassembly to aid recycling and high levels of durability, backed up by Herman Miller's 12 year three shift warranty (Herman Miller, 2005).

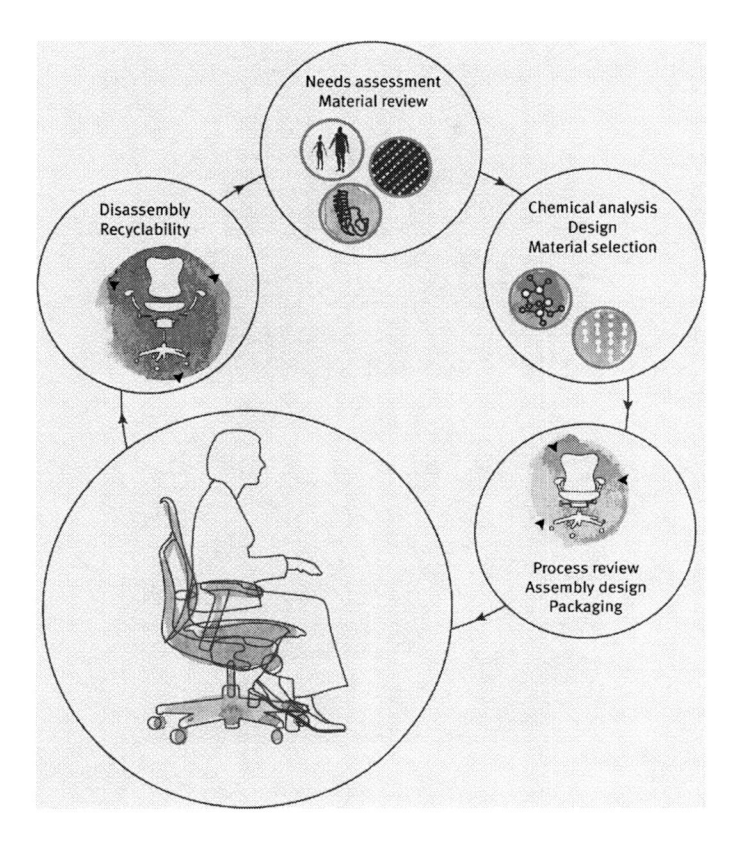

Figure 8.2 Cradle to Cradle view of the Mirra Chair

Reproduced with permission © Herman Miller Limited

Model U Ford

In 2003, a collaborative team from Ford's Research and Advanced Engineering, and Brand Imaging Group, along with Bill McDonough, BP, and a host of technology suppliers set out to tackle key questions facing the automotive industry, regarding emissions, safety and fuel economy, while incorporating green materials and processes (Ford, 2005). The result was the Model U concept (see Figure 8.3).

The Model U has a reconfigurable interior and exterior which allows for ongoing upgrades. A series of slots in the floor, door panels and instrument panel allow different components such as armrests, wireless switches or any other accessory to be mounted, moved around or added later. The slot system allows the user to take personal accessories to other vehicles, and to

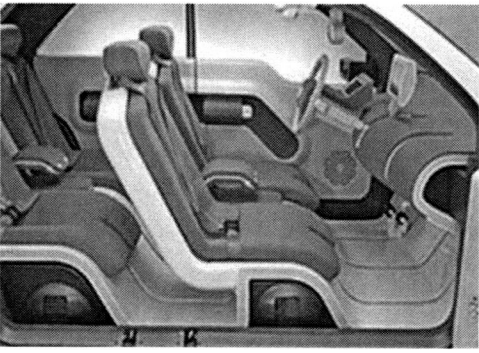

Figure 8.3 External and internal images of the Model U Ford

Reproduced with permission © Ford Motor Company Limited.

very quickly update the look of the car when it enters the used-car market. These slots are designed to provide power and access to the vehicle's electronic network enabling passengers to plug in DVD, computer or game systems. The exterior is highlighted by a power retractable roof, rear window, tailgate and trunk, allowing the vehicle to go from closed to open (Ford, 2005). Rear seats are located on slots and can be moved forward to offer more rear space or removed to create a pick up bed. Rear-seat passengers will have small entertainment screens in front of them.

The Model U is powered by a 2.3-litre, four-cylinder supercharged, intercooled hydrogen internal-combustion engine, coupled with a hybrid electric transmission (Ford, 2005). This equates to the equivalent fuel efficiency of 45 miles per gallon, a range of about 300 miles, near-zero regulated emissions and a 99 per cent reduction in carbon dioxide. The engine also features a Modular Hybrid Transmission System which allows the electric motor to simultaneously fulfil the role of the flywheel, the starter, the alternator and the hybrid traction motor (Ford, 2005). This means that when the driver stops at some traffic lights, the engine can automatically be switched off to save fuel. When the accelerator is reapplied, the electric motor instantly starts the engine and within 300 milliseconds the vehicle begins to pull away (Ford, 2005).

The Model U also integrates the most advanced conversational speech technology displayed to date, allowing the driver to speak naturally to operate on-board systems such as the entertainment, navigation, cellular telephone and climate control. It also includes a range of features to help the driver avoid accidents before they occur (media.ford.com, 2005).

The materials used in the Model U have been designed and selected for the optimum health of the car's occupants. Rather than the traditional cradle-to-grave life cycle that most materials follow, those developed for the Model U were designed to go from cradle-to-cradle, which means that they never become waste, but instead are nutrients that can either be turned into compost or fed back into the manufacturing process (Ford, 2005). They include:

- recyclable polyester on seats, dashboard, steering wheel, headrests, door trim, and armrests;
- corn-based biopolymer for the retractable canvas roof and carpet mats;
- corn-based fillers in the rubber tyres as a partial substitute for rubber black to improve rolling resistance and fuel economy;
- soy-based composite resins for the rear tailgate and side panels;
- soy-based composite foam for seating;
- interchangeable armrests for ease of maintenance and remanufacturing;
- lightweight, recyclable aluminium body (Treehugger, 2004).

EcoKitchen

In 1998, researchers at Cranfield University worked with designers at Electrolux to create the concept of the EcoKitchen. The project aimed to go beyond simply integrating environmental considerations into the product development process and chose to look at the kitchen holistically – with the aim of better exploring the product systems and relationships, rather than being limited by the restrictions of existing products (Sherwin and Bhamra, 1999). In order to develop a range of new product concepts, the team combined their understanding that the 'use' phase of the kitchen has the greatest environmental impact, with knowledge of cultural and lifestyle issues relating to dietary needs, culinary habits and how individuals interact with products. Two of the outputs are illustrated below.

The 'Data-wall' illustrated in Figure 8.4, is the brain of the kitchen. It is an information product that helps manage and communicate domestic resource use. It is connected to most kitchen products for feedback on levels of usage. Along with this it also holds an inventory of food stock, communicating quantities, freshness and use-by dates. It is a link to the supermarket for home-shopping and delivery service and contains the 'menu-master' – advice on recipes, cooking techniques and health and dietary issues. Behind this information interface is the kitchen storage, which consists of refillable and reusable containers that are designed to be cherished by the user (Sherwin and Bhamra, 1999).

The 'Smart sink' illustrated in Figure 8.5, is the centre of household water management system. A membrane sink of expanding material gets larger when filled to help minimise water use and the smart tap switches from jet to spray to mist to suit your needs. A consumption meter and a water level indicator in the main basin give feedback on rates and level of water usage. Household grey water is

Figure 8.4 Data wall

Reproduced with permission © Cranfield University/ AB Electrolux

Figure 8.5 Smart sink
Reproduced with permission © Cranfield University/ AB Electrolux

managed visibly by an osmosis purifier and a cyclone filter located in the pedestal, and linked to the household grey-water storage (Sherwin and Bhamra, 1999).

These concepts demonstrate how designers can begin to consider a systems approach to the design of products resulting in sustainability improvements. By considering the kitchen as a system rather than as individual products it was possible to create products that were interconnected and networked to share information and resources. This innovative approach would result in significant benefits from a sustainability and consumer perspective.

Carpet Tiles, InterfaceFLOR

Established in 1973, Interface Inc. has grown to become a worldwide leader in design and manufacture of commercial carpet and interior fabrics. Having recognised the environmental burden associated with the use of non-renewable fossil fuels, Interface Inc. made a commitment to reducing waste, closing material loops and shifting their focus from selling products to providing services (Anderson, 1998). InterfaceFLOR is the modular division of Interface Inc. focusing on carpet tiles.

In 1995, InterfaceFLOR launched the Evergreen Leasing system. As part of this system, the floor covering services are leased to the customer, who pays a monthly fee for the service, rather than buying carpet tiles (see Figure 8.6). InterfaceFLOR retains responsibility for the maintenance of the carpeting

Figure 8.6 InterfaceFLOR carpet tiles as used in the 'Evergreen Leasing' system

Reproduced with permission © InterfaceFLOR

throughout its lifetime; renewing and replacing damaged tiles or exchanging heavily worn tiles in areas of heavy traffic for less exposed tiles under desks or furniture. At the end of its useful life, the carpeting is recovered and is recycled, down cycled or repurposed rather than disposed of in landfill (Interface, 2006c).

Through the ReEntry system, InterfaceFLOR arranges for used carpet tiles to be retrieved. If the reclaimed tile is in good condition it is cleaned and donated to a non-profit organisation for reuse; tiles in a lesser condition are reprocessed. Interface retrieves the nylon facing, which is either recycled back into carpet tiles or down cycled to produce secondary products like moulded car parts or underlay. The backing is ground up and remanufactured into new carpet tile backing (Interface, 2006b).

In conjunction with developing service based systems, InterfaceFLOR has also continued to develop robust, sustainable products that deliver more value using less material, minimise waste, use renewable, recycled or recyclable materials, have a long lifespan and can be easily cleaned, replaced, repaired, reused or recycled. Entropy draws its design philosophy from nature. Using a biomimicry approach, Entropy simulates the random colours and patterns found in nature. Every Entropy tile is unique, therefore can be laid in a random,

Figure 8.7 Tirex carpet tiles

Reproduced with permission © InterfaceFLOR

non-directional arrangement. The random nature of the colour and pattern allows individual tiles to be easily replaced, soiling and staining to be masked and wastage reduced (Interface, 2006a).

Tirex indoor matting (see Figure 8.7) is made from 100 per cent recycled vehicle tyres. This type of product not only allows customers to make a visual statement about their commitment to environmental issues, but is also incredibly hard wearing, and has a 'classic' styling.

InterfaceFLOR's exploration of renewable resources has primarily been driven by the need to reduce dependence on fossil fuels. A key aspect in achieving this goal is their participation in the development of bio based materials. Polylactide (PLA) is a versatile, compostable polymer made using dextrose, a natural sugar derived from the starch in kernels of corn (or maize). The dextrose is fermented into lactic acid which is the basis of PLA (Dow, 2003). The fibres extruded from the PLA have been used by Interface to create yarn with which to make the face fibres of the carpet. PLA biodegrades when composted, can be burned in an incinerator or has the potential to be recycled back into lactic acid thereby diverting used carpet tiles from being disposed of in landfill sites.

One-Time-Use Video Camcorder, Pure Digital Technologies Inc

In 2005, Pure Digital Technologies Inc. of *San Francisco* introduced a Digital One-Time-Use Camcorder onto the American market (see Figure 8.8). The

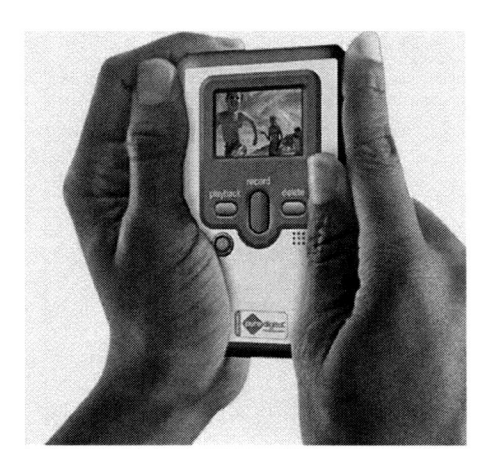

Figure 8.8   One-Time-Use Video Camcorder, Pure Digital Technologies Inc.
Reproduced with permission © Pure Digital Technologies Inc.

camcorder weighs less than 150g and is about the size of a deck of cards. It has a 35 mm square colour LCD screen that is both a viewfinder and play back screen and four buttons; on/off, play, record and delete. The lens and microphone are in front and video is recorded onto an internal 128-Mbp flash memory card which can hold up to 20 minutes of footage. The VGA camera captures images at 30 frames per second at a resolution of 640 x 480 at VHS quality enabling the user to play back and delete videos. The camcorder retails for US$30.

When the user has taken all the video they want, they return the camera to the shop where it is plugged into a computer and the video extracted and burned onto a DVD. This process takes around 30 minutes and the user receives their DVD and special software that enables them to email video clips. This processing currently costs US$13.

In order to reduce the amount of waste going to landfill and retain the financial investment they have committed to the provision of a high quality digital product, Pure Digital have designed these One-Time-Use video camcorders to be refurbished. Once the video has been extracted, they take the camera back, refurbish it if necessary and repackage it ready to be sold to another user. The company claim that they usually get about five uses out of each camcorder.

The One-Time-Use video camcorder is a product-orientated service as the user buys the product for short-term use and then returns it to the manufacturer who reuses and resells it a number of times. Some critics argue that US$30 is

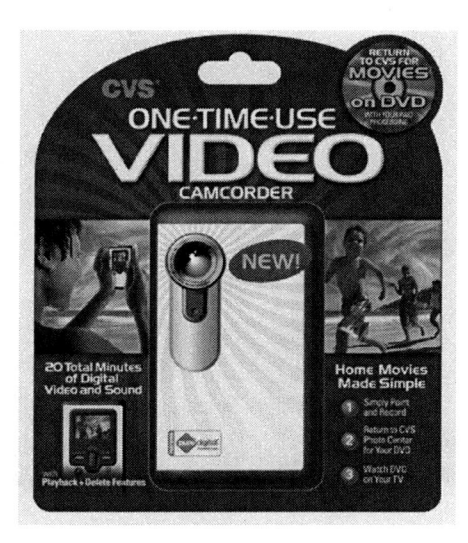

Figure 8.9 Packaging on the One-Time-Use Video Camcorder

Reproduced with permission © Pure Digital Technologies Inc.

very expensive for 20 minutes of video but the product enables people who couldn't usually afford the full purchase cost of camcorder to have the use of one when they need it. It also enables those people who do already own a camcorder to use one in an environment where they wouldn't want to take an expensive product. This product has been very successful for Pure Digital showing that the idea of paying for the use of a product can be made attractive to consumers.

Car Clubs

Throughout Europe, car clubs are becoming a popular use-orientated service which essentially allows the customer to 'pay per unit of mobility' (Manzini and Vezzoli, 2002) rather than buying a car. Customers who are members of a car club can hire a car 24 hours a day for as little as an hour at a time. Cars which are located at designated parking bays within a short walk from where customers live or work, can be booked through a central office using the telephone or Internet. Keys are either kept at a nearby safe, or in the car, which is accessed using a smart card. Drivers pay a monthly fee and are billed for hours hired and miles driven.

Car sharing intensifies the use of cars, meaning that a lower number of cars are needed for a given demand of mobility (Manzini and Vezzoli, 2002). AutoShare a Canadian corporation that provides a car-sharing service estimates

Figure 8.10 Car Clubs

Reproduced with permission © CityCarClub

that every 'shared' car on the road replaces 5–6 privately owned cars (Manzini and Vezzoli, 2002). They also found that members drove less than owners of private cars, as it is directly in their interest to reduce their hourly costs. In turn this reduced the impact of emissions. For those using a car for less than 12,000 km/year, car sharing can be cheaper than purchasing, insuring, cleaning and maintaining a private car (Manzini and Vezzoli, 2002). A successful, efficient scheme should save consumers money, reduce consumer impact in an area which is currently a high polluter, and potentially can provide greater choice for consumers. It could also be argued that schemes of this nature are socially more sustainable as they allow for a more healthy, active lifestyle by not having a car to hand for any journey.

ZED cars, the car club at BedZED (Beddington zero Energy Development) in the London Borough of Sutton was the first new development in Britain to have a car club as an integral part of the design. This helped underpin a case to reduce the usual parking provision by around 50 per cent (Carplus, 2006).

Digital Music Distribution

Until recently, ownership of recorded music has been intrinsically tied to a physical medium such as records, cassette tapes and more recently CDs (Grech and Luukkainen, 2005). However, the introduction of new encoding techniques, such as the MP3 format, coupled with the rapid development of Internet and broadband technologies, has enabled the digital distribution of music (Grech and Luukkainen, 2005).

A study which assessed the environmental impact of digital distribution identified that the digital delivery of music as compressed download files can be environmentally preferable to purchasing CDs on the high street or via online shopping, even if the files are burned onto a CD, based on the assumption that a fast Internet connection is used and that it does not lead to an increased number of music downloads (Türk et al., 2003). Interestingly, a slow Internet connection, the inefficient burning of CDs, such as using whole CD-R for a few files, and the effect of 'unselected' downloads caused by unlimited access can lead to higher resource consumption than that created by physical and online shopping (Türk et al., 2003). In other words consumer behaviour and the way in which digital music is offered to consumers strongly influences the degree to which potential savings can be made (Türk et al., 2003). Offering downloads rather than music streams and avoiding subscription models that allow unlimited access would both reduce the environmental impact (Türk et al., 2003).

From a social perspective, digital transfer of music files has created a number of positive and negative impacts. On the one hand, while access to digital music is dependent on access to a personal computer, it is unlikely to increase access to music. Reports show that patterns of digital inclusion continue to mirror patterns of social inclusion, leaving low income earners, the unemployed, disabled, and the elderly unable to afford access or without the necessary skills, confidence and motivation to get online. Yet these are the very groups who could benefit most from the wider potential of music to enable social integration through greater self expression and confidence. In addition to this public Internet access areas provided through libraries or Internet cafes do not allow files to be download and stored, and are often too outdated for listening to music (Türk et al., 2003). One potential solution may be through digital television which is proving popular with socially excluded people (Department for Education and Skills, 2001).

Digital distribution originated through websites such as Napster which facilitated the distribution of pirated content via peer-to-peer distribution networks. However, the issue of pirate music has now been tackled by the music industry through the introduction of a wide variety of legal distribution channels such as *Apple Computers' iTunes Music Store* and now Napster also provides legal downloads. Despite these many websites legally purchased

Figure 8.11 Digital music

digital music still represents a small but growing fraction of the music market (Türk et al., 2003).

Digital music also has the opportunity to promote diversity. The Internet houses a far greater diversity of music than any one provider could ever manage. The Internet can actually breathe new life into minority cultures, cross borders, and help with communication between communities. To counter this by making music accessible and appealing to the mainstream market, it can often become removed from its cultural heritage. While this can be musically innovative and bring local music to new audiences, its repercussions for local communities can be more mixed (Türk et al., 2003).

Digital technologies are also helping to remove the traditional financial barriers to musical creativity. In the past, the high cost of manufacturing, distributing and storing CDs created high barriers to entry. Digital distribution lowers barriers to entry, opening doors to musical diversity. As digital technology extends creative possibilities, so it provides opportunities via the Internet for new talent in particular to get their music heard outside of live performances (Türk et al., 2003).

In terms of social isolation there are contradictory arguments. On the one hand it can be argued that the Internet promotes participation through online communities. Artists use the Internet to reach their fans directly and involve them in the creative process. While on the other it has the potential to exacerbate social isolation as children retreat behind computer screens (Türk et al., 2003). However, there are now websites such as www.meetup.com which facilitate local meetings of interest groups, acknowledging the social potential of the Internet in promoting local interaction. Music could play an important role in bringing people together virtually as it has long done in the real world (Türk et al., 2003).

Casa Quick, Allegrini S.p.A

In 1998, Allegrini S.p.A an Italian producer of detergents and cosmetics developed Casa Quick, a service based on the home delivery distribution of biodegradable, phosphorus-free detergents.

Through Casa Quick seven different types of products are delivered each month by mobile vans, which regularly visit four municipalities (see Figure 8.12). Each family takes the detergents needed from the mobile van, in the quantity and quality preferred, using special containers and paying only for the quantity taken. Casa Quick consumers receive a special kit of plastic flasks which are easy to carry from the house to the van, and can be filled up even if not completely empty. This system incorporates the product (detergent) plus a service (home delivery), with a lower-level of customer effort. There is no need for the customer to travel to shops, rather, the shop itself comes to the customer. Information is also given to consumers on how to use the products to optimise the effect and minimise the amount used (Manzini and Vezzoli, 2002).

Allegrini's system led to both environmental and economic benefits. Environmental benefits are reaped from the optimisation of the distribution processes, in terms of both packaging and transportation. The move from disposable to refillable packaging reduced the consumption of raw materials, reduced manufacturing and dramatically reduced landfill waste. Interestingly, other problems associated with the disposal of packaging which has contained detergents, created by the possible dispersion of residual detergents, is also minimised with the Allegrini refill system (Manzini and Vezzoli, 2002).

Economic benefits are available for both the producer and consumer. Customers receive a high quality, convenient, home delivery and waste removal service that can be offered at a low price, due to the costs savings created by extending the life of the packaging. This helps to encourage long-term customer loyalty, and provides Allegrini with a competitive advantage in terms of diversification of service provided (Manzini and Vezzoli, 2002).

Figure 8.12 The Casa Quick Van

Reproduced with permission © Ecologos

In Spring 2006 Ecologos purchased the delivery van. They no longer use the Allegrini product range but have introduced new products from a small, local company called Colenghi, as they recognised that using a local operator would minimise transport pollution and support the local economy. Initially, Allegrini, were traditionally wholesalers not retailers and they decided to stop this delivery approach, because by comparison only small quantities of product were being sold. Ecologos also no longer sell cleaners 'door to door' because of the logistical problems that it created. They found that they needed a full-time employee and could only operate in a small area. Rather than delivery being made 'door to door', Ecologos usually create 4–5 days every 2 months when the van is in a specific street or square (communicated by flyers and local press). This is then supported by a range of shops which support the approach and stock the same cleaners. Ecologos also use the van for exhibitions and fairs, to support their project 'Riducimballi' – a project which aims to reduce packaging waste by promoting alternative ways of sale – in particular re-using or eliminating packaging. It initially started with cleaning products but they are also promoting the 'no-pack' sale seen with draught beer, to other products like wine, water, cereals.

Functional Sales, AB Electrolux

An interesting example of a move from product to service was illustrated by the launch of a new business pilot scheme from Electrolux on the island of Gotland in Sweden (Electrolux, 2000). The approach, called Functional Sales created a collaboration between Electrolux and the energy utility company Vattenfall.

Through the new system customers were offered a pay-per-wash option for their laundry needs (Jones and Harrison, 2000).

Instead of buying a washing machine from Electrolux, the theory was that customers would have a washing machine at home but pay for the 'function' of having clean clothes at about 72p per wash (Jones and Harrison, 2000; Jessen, 2001). This approach of paying per use would create incentives for customers to reduce their usage and hence water and detergent consumption. This, coupled with the fact that Electrolux's best washing machines consume less than 1 kWh (kilowatt/hour) and less than 40 litres of water per cycle (Jessen, 2001) would also lead to a reduction in the energy consumption (Jones and Harrison, 2000).

Through this Functional Sales pilot study, Electrolux were able to investigate the feasibility of such an approach. They identified that a shift of this nature, from product delivery to service delivery, could have significant effects on the way the product is designed. They recognised that in order for businesses to adapt to this type of model, they would have to design their products with increased endurance, serviceability and refurbishment capability. This would in turn further reduce the overall environmental impact of the product (Jones and Harrison, 2000).

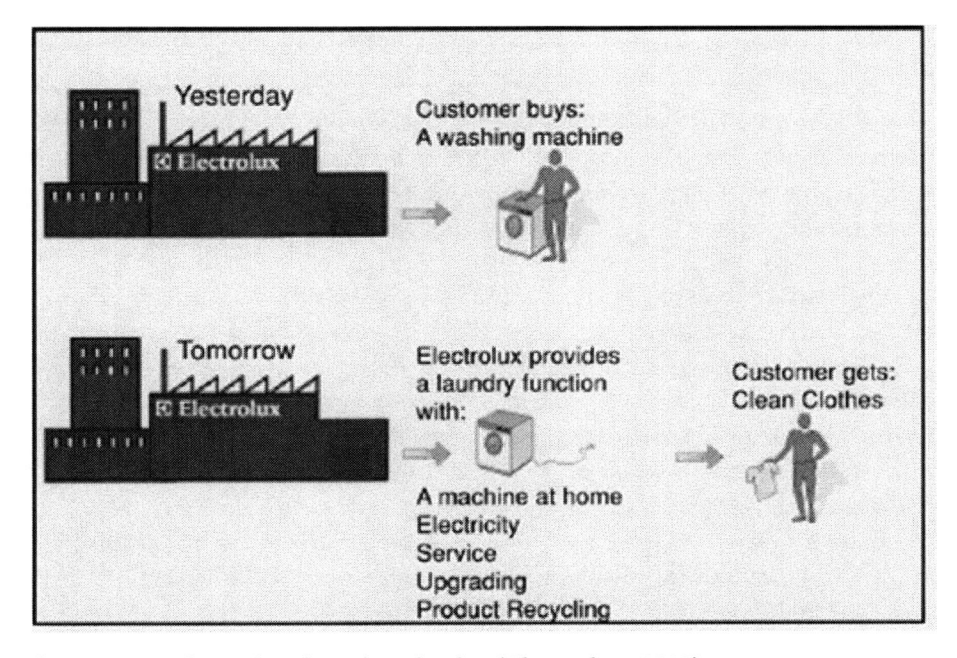

Figure 8.13 Electrolux functional sales (Electrolux, 2000)

HiCS

La Fiambrera (Lunch Box) is a food service that was developed to meet the food needs of elderly people living independently at home and employees of small companies (SMEs) based in isolated industrial estates which have no provision for food in the municipality of Rubí, near Barcelona in Spain (Jegou and Joore, 2004).

During a multidisciplinary research project called HiCS researchers used a series of context-of-use tools (Manzini et al, 2004) to explore the food requirements of the different groups. Studies showed that although the elderly did have a certain level of mobility, they had difficulties 'accessing' food because of problems with preparing it, finances, food knowledge, weight-carrying ability, agility or sight problems (Jegou and Joore, 2004). Consequently, they often eat poorly, or have to rely on outside help, which was seen to be rapidly diminishing as society becomes increasingly industrialised (Jegou and Joore, 2004). The research also identified that SME employees in isolated industrial estates often have difficulty accessing healthy lunchtime food, because of their geographical location, which resulted in either eating unhealthy snacks from petrol stations or vending machines, spending time preparing their own lunchbox, relying on a female relation to prepare their lunchbox, eating in expensive and time consuming restaurants, or not eating at lunchtime at all (Jegou and Joore, 2004).

Although both groups are very different in nature, they shared food provision needs. They both needed a regular, flexible food service, that could provide a balanced diet in a way which was easy and convenient to access and reasonably priced. The elderly group also needed a solution that would support independent living without having to rely on help from others.

La Fiambrera aimed to meet these common needs while reacting to the groups' differences (Jegou and Joore, 2004). The way that La Fiambrera works is outlined in Figure 8.14. Eurest, the catering company involved in the scheme, enters the weeks' menu into the smart ordering system on the Internet [0]. In Spain a typical lunchtime meal consists of three courses: a light vegetable, salad or pasta based dish; a meat or fish based dish; and a yoghurt, fruit or light pudding. SME employees order and pay for their lunch and any fresh food (vegetables, meats, cheeses, fish) that they require from the local municipal market, in advance through the smart ordering system [1]. SME users could also order through a feature called 'La Fiambrera de Mamá' or 'Mum's Lunchbox', which brought a surprise choice everyday (Jegou and Joore, 2004). Meanwhile,

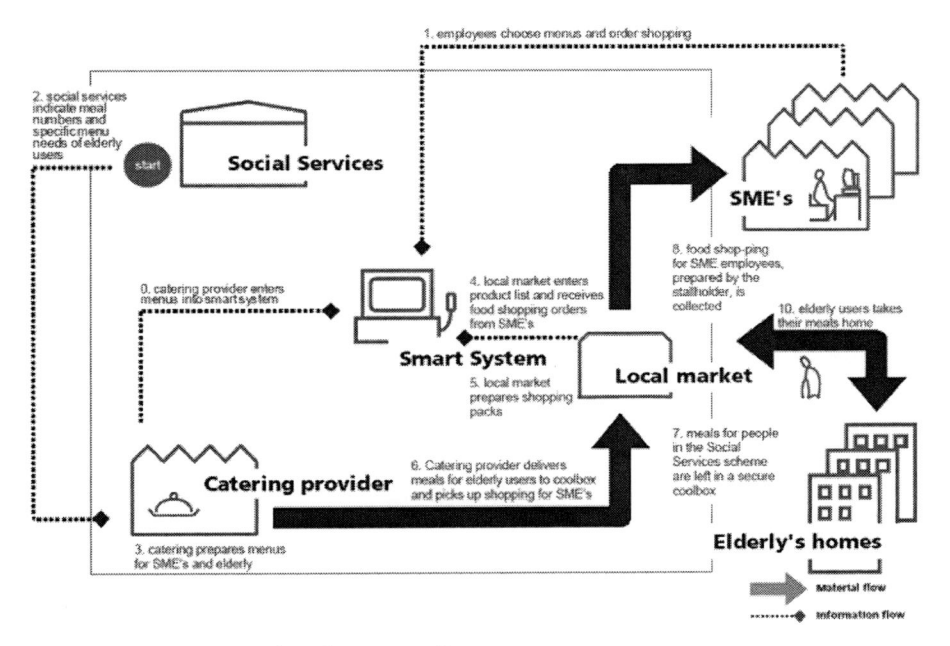

Figure 8.14 How La Fiambrera works

Reproduced with permission © Cranfield University

a social worker places an order through the Smart System for a number of set meals according to the medical needs of each elderly customer enrolled in their Scheme [2]. Meal orders go through to the Eurest Central Kitchen [3] and shopping orders go to a stallholder in the municipal market [4]. The fresh food is collected from the stalls and placed into a bag [5]. Then a van from Eurest's central kitchen carrying prepared meals for both the Social Services and SME customers goes to the municipal market. Here meals for people in the Social Services scheme are left in a secure coolbox [6], and food shopping for SME employees, prepared by the stallholder, is collected [7]. The same van then travels to the SME [9] where the prepared Eurest meals and food shopping are delivered to a coolbox. [8]. The Social Service customers walk to the municipal market to pick up their meals from the secure coolbox [9]. The food can be stored for two or three days in these fridges. Meals are packaged in individual plastic trays, with a waterproof transparent seal, that can be put directly into a microwave or oven.

The customisation of the service for users is achieved via:

- the smart ordering system which creates a user profile of food preferences and/or dietary requirements;

- the logistics which provide flexibility in access and eating times;
- the menu choices – with three options for each course per day;
- the choice of food portions – users can opt for a full menu of three dishes, or a half menu of one or two;
- the shopping – users can specify products and the quantities they want of each;
- SME employees also have the option of donating 50 cents per meal to help feed people in need of food in the local town.

La Fiambrera combines food solutions for two groups of people in one service, preparing, cooling and transporting the food together, but delivering it to different locations along one route. Information (menu posting, ordering and paying) is handled through an Internet smart system. The logistics are combined to reduce costs, making the service economically viable. La Fiambrera has helped the partners involved to reach new markets which were previously unprofitable. The concept of not only targeting more users with the same service but of adapting the service to suit different kinds of users can be seen as creating an economy of scope.

La Fiambrera has provided social services users with several social benefits. The walk to the Municipal market provides a reason to get out of the house and visit the town centre. The coolbox becomes a 'communication tool' for people

Figure 8.15 Coolboxes used in the scheme
Reproduced with permission © Cranfield University

who have not been to collect their food. Social services can be notified and can investigate to see if there is a problem.

For the SME employees La Fiambrera offers a flexible system that allows people to eat when they want. It ensures a more balanced diet and offers time savings and good quality food through a simple ordering system. It also provides a food shopping service for those who have difficulty finding time to buy fresh goods. The overriding benefit is that they now have access to a good quality food service, where previously one did not exist at all (Jegou and Joore, 2004).

Conclusions

This chapter has illustrated the concepts outlined in Chapter 7 demonstrating that taking a system or service view as part of design can bring significant environmental and social benefits. Although two of the examples highlighted in this chapter are conceptual (Eco Kitchen and Model U) and two are pilot studies (Functional Sales and La Fiambrera), they are still very valuable examples of ways in which companies and universities have rethought the traditional business model and adopted a systems or service-orientated approach to function delivery. Functional sales, digital music and the One-Time-Video camcorder all provide examples of dematerialisation, where less materials are used to deliver the same level of functionality to the user. Car clubs, the Interface examples, the One-Time-Video camcorder and La Fiambrera provide good examples of how services can intensify the use of a product, which has the effect of reducing the number of products needed. The Model U, Interface examples and the Mirra chair all use a cyclic approach, whereby nutrients are kept within a closed system and therefore the overall system impact is minimised.

Through the examples it is possible to see that this reorientation from product to service is often outside the boundaries of traditional design and is unlikely to be achieved solely by designers. Instead design of this nature is likely to require collaboration from other functions within the business. The design of systems and services can create new opportunities for collaboration between functions which have not worked together before. For example, the Casa Quick delivery service will have required much stronger collaborations between design and logistics than had ever been required previously. These case studies illustrate the breadth of design for sustainability by showing how designers can consider both environmental and social impacts in their designing and result in an innovative solution also gives benefits to the consumer.

For the case studies which still have a strong product element, it is possible to see how the design has been adapted to better suit the needs of the service or system. For example, the Casa Quick bottles were designed to be easily filled from a dispensing unit, and to be more durable than the traditional detergent packaging. In the case of the One-Time-Use video camera, the number of functions has been simplified, which is in direct contrast with the approach being adopted by manufacturers of video cameras which are sold. It is also worth noting that all of the products are more durable than their non-service counterparts.

Many of the case studies outlined in this chapter require customers to act differently, a key challenge of designing services and systems is to select markets where customers are happy to behave differently, or to identify 'value added' benefits to this new behaviour. For example, in the case of digital music, 'downloads' are cheaper than CD-based singles, can be purchased before they are available in the shops and offer the consumer more flexibility in terms of the specific songs they purchase.

The case studies in this chapter have demonstrated that there are a number of benefits to providing systems or services. The most pertinent of these are the increased opportunities for consumer loyalty, increased innovation, the opportunity to retain the value in the product, and the potential for increased positive profile.

References

Anderson, R. (1998), *Mid-Course Correction, Toward a Sustainable Enterprise: The Interface Model* (White River Junction, VT: Chelsea Green Publishing).

Carplus (2006), 'Case Studies'. Available at: www.carplus.org.uk/carclubs/case-studies.htm

Department for Education and Skills (2001), 'Cybrarian Scoping Study' (London: DfES).

Dow, C. (2003), 'NatureWorks Pla how it's Made'. Available at: www.cargilldow.com/corporate/natureworks.asp

Electrolux (2000), 'Functional Sales'. Available at: http://193.183.104.77/node323.asp

Grech, S. and Luukkainen, S. (2005), 'Towards Music Download and Radio Broadcast Convergence in Mobile Communications Networks' in *IEEE* (China: Hong Kong).

Interface (2006a), 'Entropy®'. Available at: www.interfaceflooring.com/products/sustainability/entropy.html

Interface (2006b), 'Leasing: Convenient, Cost-Effective and Sustainable'. Available at www.interfaceeurope.com/Internet/web.nsf/webpages/554_EN.html

Interface (2006c), 'Renewal: Reentry Scheme Makes a little Go a Long Way'. Available at: www.interfaceeurope.com/Internet/web.nsf/webpages/556_EN.html

Jegou, F. and Joore, P. (eds.) (2004), *Food Delivery Solutions: Cases of Solution Oriented Partnership* (Cranfield: Cranfield University).

Jessen, M. (2001), 'Clean Duds without the Washday Blues'. Available at: www.zerowaste.ca/articles/column137.html

Jones, E. and Harrison, D. (2000), 'Investigating the Use of TRIZ in Eco-Innovation' in *TRIZCON2000* (Worcester, MA: Altshuller Institute).

Manzini, E. and Vezzoli, C. (2002), *Product-Service Systems and Sustainability: Opportunities for Sustainable Solutions* (France: United Nations Environment Programme, Division of Technology Industry and Economics (DTIE)).

Manzini, E., Collins, L. and Evans, E. (eds) (2004), *Solution Oriented Partnership: How to Design Industrialised Sustainable Solutions* (Cranfield: Cranfield University).

Ford (2005), 'Model U Concept: A Model for Change'. Available at: http://media.ford.com/article_display.cfm?article_id=14047

Herman Miller (2005), 'Environmental Product Summary – Mirra Chair'. Available at: www.hermanmiller.com

Sherwin, C. and Bhamra, T. (1999), 'Beyond Engineering: Ecodesign as a Proactive Approach to Product Innovation' presented at Ecodesign '99: First International Symposium on Environmentally Conscious Design and Inverse Manufacturing, Tokyo, Japan.

Treehugger (2004), 'Ford Model U Concept SUV'. Available at: www.treehugger. com/files/2004/12/wip_ford_model.php

Türk, V., Alakeson, V., Kuhndt, M. and Ritthoff, M. (2003), *The Environmental and Social Impacts of Digital Music: A Case Study with E. M. I. Digital Europe: Ebusiness and Sustainable Development (DEESD)* (Brussels: Information Society Technologies).

Doing a Sustainable Industrial Design Project

CHAPTER

9

The ideas, tools and techniques that you have been introduced to through this book will provide you with the skills and knowledge you need to tackle a sustainable design project. However, often the biggest barrier to taking up a new challenge is knowing where to start. This chapter will pull together the ideas and themes presented in this book and offer practical advice to help you get started.

It provides useful guidance for each stage of the product development process, guiding you through the development of a socially and environmentally responsible brief, concept generation, idea development and detail design, providing guidance and suggestions on the types of environmental and social issues you should consider at each stage.

The Brief

The development of the brief is always crucially important to any design project. The brief outlines any important issues for consideration, determines what tasks need to be carried out, stipulates where responsibility lies and details the time frame. It is effectively the blueprint for the project and often the basis for any financial agreement. To be effective, sustainable design considerations need to be integrated into design practice in the same way as ergonomics, styling, manufacturing considerations and as such need to be reflected in the brief. They should also be specifically described. Rather than saying 'make it environmentally friendly', the most appropriate environmental focus for the product in question should be analysed using the Ecodesign web or Design Abacus (outlined in Chapter 5) and specific features for improvement should be identified. For example, for a mobile phone the focus could be to reduce its energy consumption during use and to ensure that it complies with the WEEE Directive (see Chapter 3). In order to achieve these requirements the resulting product would have to be designed for disassembly and recycling.

The brief setting stage is usually led by senior management, influenced by the strategic plan for the company, and often heavily influenced by marketing (Eckert and Stacey, 2000; Sherwin, 2000). It involves the identification of a list of market and technical requirements, which are presented as a formal or informal brief, or design specification. In the early stages of a project the brief can be a very short statement. This may be because the client is uncertain about what is wanted, or because they assume the designer understands exactly what is wanted. The nature and degree of flexibility available in a brief will depend on whether the client is commissioning a 'concept' or 'core' design project. The different considerations and opportunities for both type of design project are described below.

CONCEPT DESIGN PROJECT

Concept design projects are ultimately about developing something 'new'. Many student projects fall into this category, but industrial projects can equally be conceptual or 'blue-sky'. A brief for a conceptual project almost always has more potential for flexibility and wider thinking. When developing this type of brief it is important to work with the client as early as possible to ensure that the language used to discuss the project does not limit the opportunities available. For example, rather then developing a concept for a new mobile phone it might be better to consider a concept for a new communication device. By reframing the problem and taking a broader focus, designers have a greater opportunity to think differently about the design outcome and not necessarily focus immediately on developing a standard product. This can open up the potential for integrating a service element and generating new ways of delivering function to the customer as was illustrated by the One-Time-Use Video Camcorder outlined in Chapter 8.

Early intervention from an educated designer can also help to orientate a new concept towards consumer 'needs' rather than consumer 'wants', the importance of which was outlined in Chapter 4. This element of developing a sustainable brief may prove to be the most challenging, as meeting fundamental human 'needs' rather than whimsical wants might not necessarily align with the requirements of marketing. Designers need to understand that it is their responsibility to use their design skills to move the client towards sustainability. Ultimately, if a client asks you to develop a product which you consider to be wholly unsustainable and you are unable to steer the direction of the brief through discussion, you could take the decision to refuse the commission.

CORE DESIGN BRIEF

Core design projects are redesign projects which focus on revamping, updating, and/or tweaking an existing product to make it better. In terms of addressing sustainability, the starting point for this type of project is often to reflect on the brief to ensure that it focuses on social and/or environmental issues specifically. Social improvements could include:

- making the product easier for the consumer to use, and
- making it inclusive.

Environmental improvements could include

- making it easier and more cost-effective to disassemble,
- giving it an alternate energy source which does not rely on fossil fuels, and
- eliminating the use of toxic substances.

A brief clarification meeting between the designer and client at the very early stages of a project provides an ideal opportunity for designers to investigate these areas further. For example, at a client meeting to discuss the brief illustrated in Figure 9.1 the designer might traditionally question the client about what is meant by the term 'reliable', what standard of reliability is currently attained, how this is measured, and what level of reliability is acceptable?

A motivated designer might go beyond this and ask – what would make refillable packaging appeal to the young family? What do young families actually need? What is known about the level of manual dexterity required for young

---

Design spec for refillable shower gel pack

⇒ Total retail price £3 (product and package)
⇒ Aimed at young family to be bought by young mum
⇒ Attractive to suit a modern bathroom environment
⇒ As reliable in delivery as standard packaging
⇒ Size not to exceed 2 or 3 times the volume of the refill container
⇒ To create convenient, value added brand experience

Figure 9.1 Sample brief for a shower gel pack

people to use the product effectively? Would some materials be more appropriate to this type of packaging than others? How does the client anticipate the refill system working? What will happen to the refills and the refill container at the end of its life? Designers need to meet with a range of stakeholders to understand the problem context, before they can start to build the brief – especially if they are involved in a complex product/service problem.

These additional questions can either be seen as the designer taking the opportunity to educate the client about considering socially and environmentally responsible thinking or they can be seen as asking the right questions to ensure that product development is as good as it can be. Depending on the open-mindedness of the client, the designer can decide whether to make this education implicit or explicit. Explicit education would start to highlight the benefits sustainable thinking can bring, such as improved customer relations, increased brand value and reduced manufacturing costs.

The easiest way for sustainable design to get into the brief is for the 'pull' to come from the client. However, even if this is not forthcoming the growing raft of environmentally focused legislation such as EC Packaging and Packaging Waste Directive 94/62/EC, the European Waste Electrical and Electronic Equipment Directive and the anticipated Directive 2005/32/EC on the eco-design of Energy-using Products (EuP) (see Chapter 3), will provide knowledgeable designers in large organisations and consultancies alike with the opportunity to 'push' environmentally responsible thinking through the design supply chain, by helping companies to meet their legal obligations. This new design focus will enable teams to offer an additional value added service.

Concept Generation

Once the brief has been formulated the project moves into the concept generation stage where the aim is to generate new ideas and concepts of a technical and non-technical nature. User orientated research carried out by the design team or external agencies needs to feed into this stage. Industrial designers will then focus on developing new product concepts to challenge and complement strategic business (Svengren, 1997; Tovey, 1997, Sherwin, 2000) and design engineers tend to focus on developing new technological innovations that can be integrated into product development at a later date (Electrolux Technology Group, 1997). At this stage the design process is rapid and interactive. Once industrial designers have been given a brief for a project, they 'pick it up and run with it'. They use mood boards to stimulate and contextualise design, and to create a 'sense' of the product. This stage typically involves the production of sketches and drawings, and mock-ups in blue foam or cardboard to test basic technical feasibility.

During the concept generation stage designers have the opportunity to consider the bigger picture. This might involve considering opportunities for designing a closed loop reuse and recycling system such as the one developed by Kodak where they manage the impact of the system by controlling the product lifespan (see Chapter 8). It might involve integrating high quality multiple functions into one product to reduce the number of products required, as was the case with the development of the mobile phone with built-in camera, video, diary and satellite navigation. This is a good time to consider the durability of the product and investigate different lifespan options. It might involve dematerialisation as in the case of digital music distribution or a move from a product to a product and service mix such as in the case of car clubs (see Chapter 8). It could also involve making statements about issues such as anti-fashion and anti-consumption, as illustrated by the British clothing company, Howies (www.howies.co.uk).

During this stage ideas are generated through the use of individual and group brainstorming sessions. Creativity techniques such as 'Random Words', 'What If' and 'Forced Relationships' (introduced in Chapter 5) are useful at this

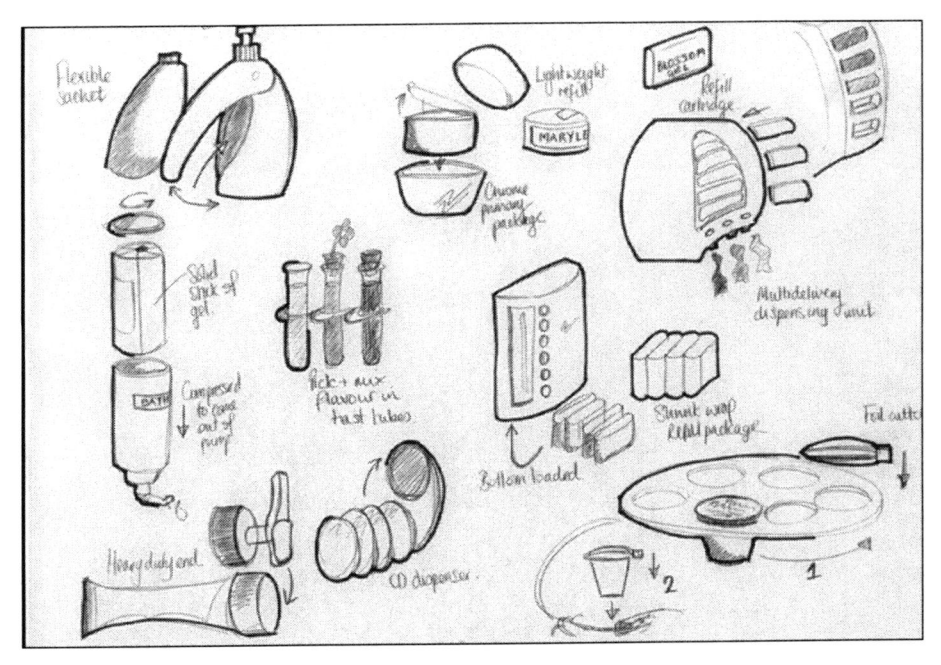

Figure 9.2 Concepts for refillable shower gel packaging

stage and also help teams to think about things differently. In addition to these approaches, the Flowmaker cards can help teams to look at a problem from a different angle, or focus more carefully on specific issues. This concept generation stage generally results in the production of one or more design concepts which may or may not be based in reality (see Figure 9.2). The concepts are fed into the next stage of the product development process – idea development.

Idea Development

At this stage in the product development process, the design is developed and scope is added to the project. Designers explore a wide range of alternatives, investigating them through 2D sketches, 3D card models, CAD models, layout drawings, schematics and mock-ups.Mock-ups and/or prototypes will be used to test technical principles (such as usability and manufacturing capabilities), visualise layouts and ensure that styling encourages a certain use. For the refillable packaging brief introduced earlier, the idea development stage would involve the configuration of the various components, performance calculations and decisions on materials and finishes (see Figure 9.3).

During the idea development stage designers need to identify the strategies which they are going to focus on to reduce the environmental and social impact of the product. This might include identifying opportunities for using alternative

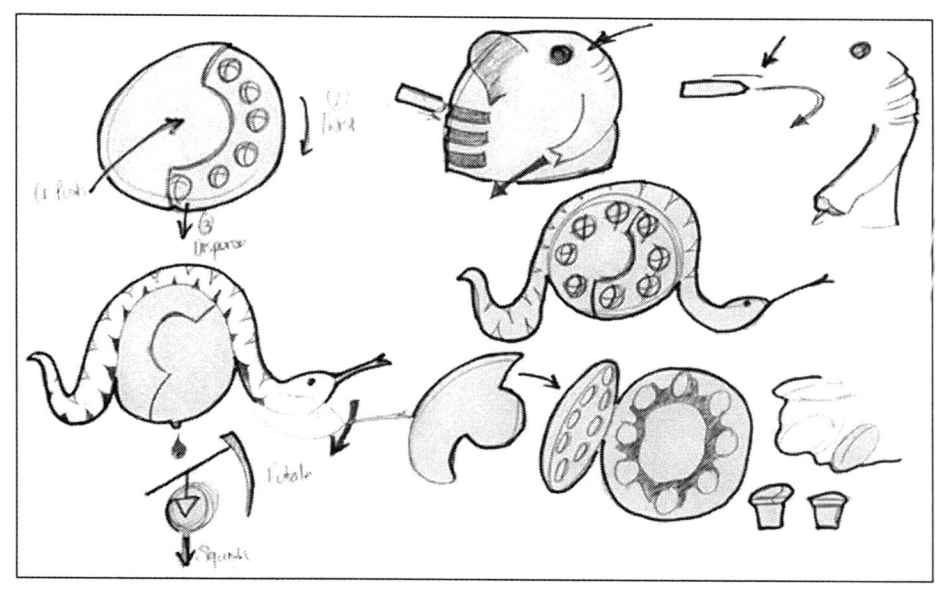

Figure 9.3   Example sketches produced at the idea development stage

energy sources. It might involve considering improved usability, some form of user education or mechanisms for reducing the negative social impacts of a product. In terms of materials it might involve identifying materials which will have less environmental impact (recycled, renewable) or those which are most easily recycled. The information part of the 'Information/Inspiration' web resource – www.informationinspiration.org.uk – provides links to a whole range of strategies that you can draw on to improve the performance of your products and the Ecodesign Web and Eco Indicator tools can provide a structure to work through to help you identify key areas to focus on.

During the idea development stage designers often take their competitors products apart to see how they are manufactured and how they work. This activity directly complements sustainable design practice and provides the opportunity for designers to better understand assembly and disassembly practices and to investigate how a product can be improved from an end of life perspective. This might include investigating techniques for marking materials, reducing the number and type of plastics used, reducing the number of materials used, and identifying areas in the product where lower grade (cheaper) recycled materials can be incorporated. Discussions with manufacturing suppliers about these issues can be very useful at this stage.

Detail Design

At the detail design stage industrial designers use manufacturing and material knowledge, to design product concepts that are efficient and profitable to produce (Svengren, 1997; Tovey, 1997) and issues such as safety and usability are further refined. The lessons learnt from the idea development stage such as lightweighting the mouldings, reducing energy consumption, improving disassembly can be fed into the detail design stage. By the end of the stage, the working drawings (as illustrated in Figure 9.4) that provide information on the materials selected, tolerances and manufacturing processes, are passed onto the production engineers. At this point it is generally too late (and too expensive) to make any further changes to the design.

Moving Forward

This book has demonstrated that design for sustainability has come a long way since the 1970s and is now high on the business agenda. Sustainability is also rising on the consumers horizon – with an increase of 46 per cent in sales of Fair Trade products (Fairtrade Foundation, 2007), an increase in the availability and purchase of sustainable technologies (Coughlan, 2006), in response to

Generating a Brief for a Student Project

If you are trying to generate a sustainable design brief for a school or university project there are a number of techniques that you can use to help you.

Brainstorm as many different potential sources of ideas as you can – music, sport, travel, cinema, office work, stay-at-home mums/dads, parenthood, travel, holidays, school, nursery, old people's homes, entertainment, music. Create a list of people and organisations that you could speak to. Is there a charity that you can contact that could provide you with inspiration such as Practical Action, Oxfam or WWF? Is there a local business or organisation that you could solve a design problem for? Consider which groups of individuals you could interview to identify needs which you had previously been unaware of – children, the elderly, the infirm, tall people, short people, parents, pet owners, self-employed people, office workers, farmers, shop keepers – the list goes on. Arrange to speak to the people that you want to design for – talk to in more detail about the issues which affect them on a daily basis. Identify what would make their lives easier.

Seek creativity by reading something you wouldn't normally read – *New Scientist*, *Knitting Weekly*, *Design Week*, *Home and Living*, *Cosmopolitan*, *FACE*, *The Beano*, *Conté Nast Traveler*. Type random words into an Internet search engine, see what you find. Visit places you don't normally go – a show, the Design Museum, your local library, a local museum, a car boot sale, an auction, a market, the countryside, a high class restaurant, the Tower of London, the races, the pub, the supermarket. Keep your eyes open and allow yourself to draw inspiration from new surroundings and from watching people. Can you identify problem areas? Drawing inspiration from people, places and experiences that you do not usually experience can be an amazing source of inspiration. IDEO have produced a great book called 'Thoughtless acts' (Suri and IDEO, 2005) which provides about 150 pages of images to show the different ways that we unconsciously interact with products. This can be great inspiration for the products we design.

Surf around 'Information/Inspiration' www.informationinspiration.org.uk and allow yourself to be inspired by the sustainable design work that others have done before you. Visit other sustainable design education websites such as the Sustainable Design Awards website (www.sda-uk.org) for further inspiration.

Once you have opened yourself up to a wide range of new experiences and given yourself the opportunity to generate new ideas sit down with a large piece of paper and write down any ideas that you have for projects. At this stage don't be critical! Give all of your ideas paper space – turn the page over, put it to one side and write some more ideas down. Can you link any of your ideas together?

It is now time to make a decision. Circle your favourite ideas and use the feasibility assessment grid in Chapter 5 to analyse them.

Finally, if you are trying to generate a brief for a final year degree programme, it would also be useful to identify what skills you want your final project to demonstrate. Identify what you are good at and what you enjoy doing and try to build these elements into the project so that you provide yourself with the best opportunity to showcase your skills.

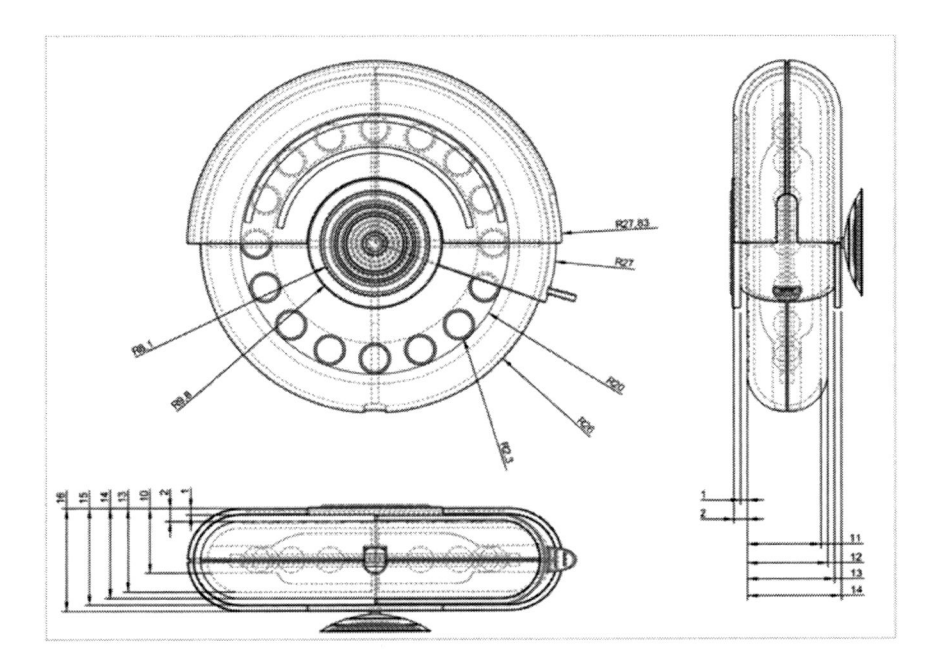

Figure 9.4 Example of an assembly drawing

increasing energy bills and the introduction of additional taxes on air travel (BBC News, 2007). In a changing world where consumers are beginning to expect socially and environmentally responsible products, and supermarkets carry slogans such as 'We go further so that you don't have to', sustainability is a greater priority for designers. This has been further enhanced by a new raft of environmental legislation which has moved beyond focusing on just the manufacturing impact of products, to focusing on the way a product is designed and its impact in use and at the end of its life.

In response to this, a broader suite of more appropriate resources and tools have been developed to support designers (see Chapter 5) and products from the likes of Hewlett Packard, Philips and Miele help to show what is possible. Reaching further, a range of concept projects help to demonstrate what might one day be possible – such as the 'Disappearing-Pattern Tiles' which aimed to communicate energy usage to the user (Lagerkvist et al., 2005). Decorated with patterns in a thermo-chromic ink that reacts to heat and fade away to reflect splashes and the intensity of hot water use. This concept developed as part of the STATIC! Project, aimed to use the surface of the tile as a subtle reminder of personal energy use, by reflecting the duration and waste of water consumed during a shower (Lagerkvist et al., 2005).

Thinking is also progressing beyond the realms of products and investigating new ways of doing things. Chapter 7 illustrated how design can move beyond designing individual products to begin to address the development of more sustainable systems as a whole and therefore enables greater sustainability gains to be made. In addition design is now beginning to focus on services as well as products to enable consumers to get their needs fulfilled with less material resources and product ownership. Consequently this broader scope is likely to lead to an increased requirement for design teams to work with a broader range of stakeholders such as purchasing and logistics.

The authors of this book believe that there are two key factors to successfully involving designers in ecodesign and design for sustainability – education and information. Reading this book will have raised your sensitivity and awareness to the types of issues that you should be considering when developing a product. This raised awareness will help to motivate you to ask the right questions. The tools and techniques that you will have picked up along the way will help you to tackle the challenges more effectively. The challenge for the future is to try and ensure that as designers we take responsibility for our actions and continue to ride the green wave. As a profession we need to be proactive and move beyond the requirements of legislation and focus on identifying the most appropriate ways of fulfilling our human needs. Sustainable design issues need to remain on the radar and become the norm, rather than a transient fad.

References

BBC News (2007), 'Q&A: Air Passenger Tax Rise'. Available at: http://news.bbc.co.uk/1/hi/uk/6258327.stm

Coughlan, S. (2006), 'Power from the People' in *BBC NEWS Magazine*. Available at: http://news.bbc.co.uk/1/hi/magazine/4785488.stm

Eckert, C. and Stacey, M. (2000), 'Sources of Inspiration: a Language of Design', *Design Studies*, **21**, pp. 523–538. [DOI: 10.1016/S0142-694X%2800%2900022-3].

Electrolux Technology Group (1997), *The Integrated Product Development Process* (Stockholm: AB Electrolux).

Fairtrade Foundation (2007), 'Fairtrade Spreads across the Nation as Over 250 Towns Say "Change Today, Choose Fairtrade"'. Available at: www.fairtrade.org.uk/pr280207.htm

Lagerkvist, S., von der Lancken, C., Lindgren, A. and Sävström, K. (2005), 'Disappearing-Pattern Tiles'. Available at: www.tii.se/static/disappearing.htm (Sweden: STATIC!).

Sherwin, C. (2000), 'Innovative Ecodesign - An Exploratory and Descriptive Study of Industrial Design Practice' In *School of Industrial and Manufacturing Science* (Cranfield: Cranfield University).

Suri, J. F. and I. D. E.O. (2005), *Thoughtless Acts?* (San Francisco: Chronicle Books).

Svengren, L. (1997), 'Industrial Design as a Strategic Resource: A Study of Industrial Design Methods and Approaches for Companies Strategic Development', *The Design Journal*, **10**, pp. 3–11.

Tovey, M. (1997), 'Styling and Design: Intuition and Analysis in Industrial Design', *Design Studies*, **18**, pp. 5–31 [DOI: 10.1016/S0142-694X%2896%2900006-3].

Hazardous Materials

APPENDIX 1

Substances banned or restricted under the RoHS Directive

Table A1.1 Substances banned or restricted under RoHS[1]

Banned/Restricted Substance	Use/Where Found in Electronics
Cadmium	Batteries, paints, yellow pigment, plastics additives (especially PVC used in cable assemblies), phosphorescent coatings, detectors/devices/LEDs
Mercury	Switches, pigments, paints, polyurethane materials (high gloss windows), lamps, bulbs/lighting (displays, scanners, projectors)
Hexavalent Chromium	Metal finishes for corrosion protection (chasses, fasteners), aluminum conversion coatings, alloys, pigments paints
Polybrominated Biphenyls (PBBs)	Flame retardants (plastics, housings, cables, connectors, fans, components, paints)
Polybrominated Diphenyl Ethers (PBDE)	Same as PBBs
Lead	Solder and interconnects, batteries, paints, pigments, piezoelectric devices*, discrete components, sealing glasses, CRT glass*, PVC cables (UV/heat stabiliser), metal parts, chasses, washers

PRODUCT EXCEPTIONS

Aside from selected medical equipment and industrial tools, the only other exception permitted under RoHS involves replacement parts. The directive allows producers to supply 'original equipment' or otherwise non-conforming replacement parts at any time to repair a non-conforming product that was sold into the market prior to the implementation of RoHS. Non-conforming replacement parts cannot be used to repair products that conform with RoHS, regardless of when they were sold.

FURTHER INFORMATION

Part V draft regulations – DTI RoHS regulations – Government Guidance notes – Consultation draft, July 2004 – http://www.dti.gov.uk/sustainability/weee/RoHS_Regs_Draft_Guidance.pdf

WEEE Directive

Substances which have to be removed prior to disposal, as a result of the WEEE Directive. This includes the removal of:

- mercury which can be used in components such as switches,
- batteries
- printed circuit boards (PCB) greater than 10 cm^2
- toner cartridges, liquid and pasty, as well as colour toner
- plastic containing brominated flame retardants
- asbestos waste and components which contain asbestos
- cathode ray tubes
- chlorofluorocarbons (CFC), hydrochlorofluorocarbons (HCFC) or hydrofluorocarbons (HFC), hydrocarbons (HC)
- gas discharge lamps
- liquid crystal displays (together with their casing where appropriate) greater than 100 cm^2 and all those back-lighted with gas discharge lamps
- external electric cables
- components containing refractory ceramic fibres
- components containing radioactive substances with the exception of components that are below the exemption thresholds
- electrolyte capacitors containing substances of concern (height > 25 mm, diameter > 25 mm or proportionately similar volume).[2]

References

[1] The Milwaukee Electronics Companies (2005), *Understanding* the *Requirements* of the *European RoHS Directive* and *its Impact* on *Your Business* and *PCB*

Assembly. Available at: www.meccompanies.com/european-rohs-pcb-assembly.html

[2] European Parliament and The Council of the European Union (2003), Directive (2002/96)/EC of the European Parliament and of the Council of 27 January 2003 on Waste Electrical and Electronic Equipment (WEEE). In *Official Journal of the European Union*.

Index

References to pages with illustrations are in bold

A
3 R measures 30
anti-globalisation 2
appropriate technology 10
Arts and Crafts Movement, UK 2

B
Batteries Directive 33–4
Bauhaus design school, Germany 2
Berlin Wall collapse (1989) 1
Bhopal disaster (1984) 1
biodiversity, recognition 11
brief *see* design brief
Brundtland Report (1987) 9, 11–12
brushes, sustainable 114, **115**, 116
business, and sustainable development 23–35
business case, for sustainable development 23–4
business response, to sustainable development 24–30

C
camcorder, one-time-use 147, **148**, **149**, 164
camera, single use 105, **106**
capital
    financial 26
    human 26
    manufactured 26
    natural 25
    social 26
car clubs 149, **150**
carpet tiles 145, **146**, **147**
Carson, Rachel, *Silent Spring* 9
Carter, Jimmy 11
Centre for Sustainable Design 4
CFC gases, and the ozone layer 10–11
chair **110**, 111–13
    cradle to cradle design 139, **140**, **141**
Chernobyl disaster (1986) 1
Club of Rome, *Limits to Growth* 10
coffee vending machine, MET Matrix 68–69
consumables, recycling 48
consumers, behaviour steering 49–50
corporate social responsibility 24–5
    philanthropy, distinction 25
cradle to cradle
    chair design 139, **140**, **141**
    design for sustainability 121–2
    fabric design 122
creativity techniques 78, **79**, 81, 87–8
    forced relationships 83–5
    random words 83
    'what if?' 83
CRTs, recycling 55

D
DDT effects 9
Dell Inspiron, development 37
dematerialisation, music example 125
DEMI project 4
design, priorities for 56
    see also Industrial Design
Design Abacus 71, 72, **73–4**, 75, **76**, 163
design brief
    conceptual projects 164
    contents 164
    core design projects 165–6
    design for sustainability in 4
    function 163
    generation, techniques 170

for Industrial Revolution 5–6
product development 163–6
refusal 164
shower gel pack 165
design for sustainability
    advantages 28–30, 38–9
    case studies 103–19, 139–60
    cradle to cradle 121–2
    in design brief 4
    and eco-design 39–40
    emergence 3–4
    features 5
    legislation 30–4
    methods/tools 65–100
        creativity techniques
            78, **79**, 81, 87–8
        Design Abacus 71, 72,
            73–4, 75, **76**, 163
        Eco-Indicator 70–2, 99
        Ecodesign Web 72, **73–4**, 163
        environmental assessment 65–72
        Fast five 75–7
        Flowmaker 80–1, **82**
        idea generation 78–86
        information provision 95–9
        'Information/Inspiration'
            78, **79**, 95, **96**, 168
        layered games 92–3
        lifecycle assessment 65–7
        MET Matrix 67–69
        model **66**
        'Money Talks' template 92, **93**
        mood boards 94, **94**, 95
        participant observation 87, **88**
        product-in-use **90**, 90–1
        RealPeople 95, **97–8**
        scenario-of-use 91
        six rules of thumb 77–8
        strategic design 71–8
        user-centred design 86–95
        user trials 88–9, **89**
    prizes for 4
    progress 169, 171–2
    research 5
    services approach 123–33
    system innovation 122, **123**
    systems approach 121–3
designers
    challenge for 5
    and eco-services 133

energy sources, selection 46
lifestyle choices, influence on 37–8
materials selection 41–5
    see also materials
product development,
    influence on 37, **38**
and sustainable behaviour 38
vagueness of term 2
detergents, biodegradable 153, **154**
diapers *see* nappies
Dow Jones Sustainability Group
    Indexes 12, 35

E
e-waste reduction, targets 32–3
Earth Council, established (1992) 12
Earth Summit, Rio (1992) 9, 12, 13–14
eco-design
    and design for sustainability 39–40
    philosophies 40
eco-efficiency 23, 27–8
    objectives 28
eco-feedback
    Kambrook Axis kettle 48
    Viridian light switch 48–9
Eco-Indicator 99
    design tool 70–2
        electric juicer example 71–2
eco-services 126
    for and against 132
    designers, implications for 133
    drivers 130–1
    environmental effects 131–3
    obstacles 131
Ecobottle 106, **107**, 108
Ecodesign Web 72, **73–4**, 163
    Isotonic drink bottle **74**
EcoKitchen 143, **144**, 145
Electrolux 4, 41, 118, 143, 166
    washing machine, pay-
        per-wash 154, **155**
ELV Directive 31
energy
    efficiency 47
    solar 46, **47**
    sources 46
Energy using Product (EuP)
    Directive 34, 166
Environmental Space 19
    UK targets 20

EU, sustainability legislation 30
EU Directives
    Batteries 33–4
    ELV 31
    Energy using Product (EuP) 34, 166
    Packaging and Packaging
        Waste 33, 166
    RoHS 44, 175
    WEEE 31–3, 44, 51, 55, 163, 166, 176

F
fabric design, cradle to cradle 122
Fair Trade products 169, 171
Fast five design tool 75–7
First Earth Day (1970) 10
Five Capitals model 25–6
Flowmaker design tool 81–2, **83**
food service 156, **157**, **158**, 159
Forum for the Future 25
    Sustainability Pays 23
Friends of the Earth 1
    established 9–10
FTSE 4 Good Index Series 12, 35
furniture transport, packaging 113, **114**

G
Germany, Bauhaus design school 2
Global 2000 Report (1981) 11
Global Strategy for Health
    for All (1981) 11
global warming 11
Green Movement 1
Greenpeace 1
    established 10
    Innogy, partnership 2

H
hazardous materials, RoHS Directive 175
human needs
    Maslow's hierarchy 56–7
    Max-Neef's satisfiers 57–8, 59

I
income inequality **16**, 18
Industrial Design 1–2, 56
    forces influencing **3**
Industrial Design Society of America 2
Industrial Revolution, design brief 5–6

'Information/Inspiration', design
    tool 78, **79**, 95, **96**, 168
Innogy, Greenpeace, partnership 2
Intergovernmental Panel on
    Climate Change 12
International Council of
    Scientific Unions 11
iron (domestic) **108**, 109

J
Japan, Home Appliance Recycling Law 30
juicer, Eco-Indicator 99 71–2

K
kettle, eco-feedback 48
Kyoto Protocol (1997) 12

L
labelling systems, recycling 55
layered games 93–4
legislation
    design for sustainability 30–4
    EU 30
    Japan 30
LiDS wheel 72
lifecycle
    assessment tools 65–7
    products **39**, 40–1
lifestyle
    designers' influence on 37–8
    meaning 37–8
light switch, eco-feedback 48–9

M
McDonald's, Natural Step Framework 27
Maslow, Abraham, human
    needs hierarchy 56–7
materials
    biodegradable 42
    hazardous 44, 175
    mainstream 42
    quantity, reduction 45
    recycled 43–4
    renewable 43
    selection, by designers 41–5
    variety, reduction of 44–5
Max-Neef, M.A., human needs
    satisfiers 57–8, 59

MET Matrix design tool 67–9
   coffee machine 70–1
metals, recycling 54
Miele washing machine 103, **104**, 105
mobile phone
   case, biodegradable 42, **43**
   design 163
   energy use 67
   recyclable 117, **118**
Model U Ford car, design 141, **142**, 143
'Money talks' game 93, **94**
monitored dosing system,
   packaging **109**, 110
Montreal Protocol (1987) 11
mood boards 94, **95**, 96
music distribution 150–1, **152**, 153

N
nappies, cloth vs disposable 67
Natural Step Framework 26–7
   in McDonald's 27

O
oil crisis, OPEC (1973) 10
ozone layer
   and CFC gases 10–11
   hole discovered 11

P
packaging
   furniture transport 113, **114**
   monitored dosing system **109**, 110
Packaging & Packaging Waste
   Directive 33, 166
Papanek, Victor 1, 2, 3, 55–6
participant observation 88–9, **89**
PCBs, recycling 55
philanthropy, corporate social
   responsibility, distinction 25
Philips 4, 46, 47, 77, 116
   Azur Precise Iron **108**, 109
   iU22 ultrasound system 116, **117**
plastics 42
   recycling 54–5
Polluter Pays Principle 10
pollution
   prevention 24
   and sustainable development 18

poverty, and sustainable
   development 18, 19
Practical Action charity 4, 10
product development
   the brief 163–6
      generation of 170
   concept generation 166–8
      shower gel packaging **167**
   Dell Inspiron 37
   designers' influence on 37, **38**
   detail design 169, **171**
   idea development 168, **169**
product-in-use **90**, 90–1
products
   behaviour steering, consumers 49–50
   components reuse 54
   dematerialisation 125
   design-focused approaches 45–8
   disassembly 51–2
      active 53
      automated 52
      manual 52–3
      mechanical 52
      smart materials use 53
   dual functionality 47
   durability, benefits of 50–1
   eco-feedback 48–9
   energy
      recovery 55
      source 46
   and human needs 56–9
   impact of use 45–50
   intelligent 49, 53
   lifecycle 40–1, 58
      elements **39**
      end of 51–5
      increasing 50
      limiting 51
   needs-focused approach 55–60
      see also human needs
   recycling 54–5
   remanufacturing 53–4
   services
      comparison 125–6, 127
      move to 124–5, 159–60
   user-focused approaches 48–50

R
RealPeople 95, **97–8**

recycling
    consumables 48
    CRTs 55
    labelling systems 55
    metals 54
    PCBs 55
    plastics 54–5
    products 54–5
Robert, Kark Henrik 26
RoHS Directive 44
    banned substances 175

S
scenario-of-use 92
Schumacher, Fritz, *Small is Beautiful* 10
services
    approaches 123–33
        summary 130
    concepts **128**
    eco-services 126
    product-oriented 127–8
    products
        comparison 125–6, 127
        move from 124–5
    results-oriented 129
    user-oriented 128–9
    see also eco-services
Shape Memory Alloys (SMA) 53
Shape Memory Polymers (SMP) 53
Shell 2
shower gel pack
    concepts **167**
    design brief 165
six rules of thumb, design tool 78
Sony 46
STEP programme, UK 4
Stockholm Conference (1972) 10
Strong, Maurice 10
sustainability
    in UK National Curriculum 4
    waves 1–2
    see also sustainable development
sustainability index, global 12
sustainable behaviour, designers' influence 38
Sustainable Design Awards, UK 4
sustainable development
    and business 23–35
        business case 23–4
    business response 24–30
    changes needed 19–20
    definition 9
    drivers, emerging 19
    economies
        developed 17
        emerging 18
        survival 18
    key events 9–14
    objectives 13
    obstacles to 16–19
    and pollution 18
    and poverty 18, 19
    principles 14–15
        Environmental Justice 14
        Equity Today 14
        Intergenerational Equity 14
        Stewardship 15
    'three pillars' 15–16
        economic prosperity 15
        environmental quality 15
        social equality 15–16
    and women 19
    see also design for sustainability
Sustainable Development Strategy, UK 12–13
system innovation 122, **123**
systems approach 121–3

T
table, outdoor **47**
technology, appropriate 10
Toolbox for Sustainable Design 4
treeplast 43, **44**

U
UK
    Arts and Crafts Movement 2
    Environmental Space targets 20
    STEP programme 4
    Sustainable Design Awards 4
    Sustainable Development Strategy 12–13
ultrasound system 116, **117**
UN Commission on Sustainable Development (1993) 12
UN Conference on Environment and Development (1992) (Earth Summit) 9, 12, 13–14

UN Conference on Human Environment (1972) 10
UN Environment Programme (UNEP) 10, 11
UN World Charter for Nature (1982) 11
UN World Commission on Environment and Development established (1983) 11
  Our Common Future (Brundtland Report) 9, 11–12
US, sustainability legislation 30–1
user trials 88–9, **89**

V
vehicles, end of life Directive 31
Viridian light switch, eco-feedback 48–9

W
washing machine 103, **104**, 105

pay-per-wash 154, **155**
WEEE Directive 31–3, 44, 51, 55, 163, 166, 176
  removable substances 176
wind power, Juice brand 2
women, and sustainable development 19
World Business Council for Sustainable Development 23
  Changing Course 12
World Conservation Strategy (1980) 11
World Economic Forum 2
World Meteorological Society 11
World Social Forum 2
World Summit for Social Development (1995) 12
World Summit on Sustainable Development 13–14

X
Xerox, product-oriented service 128

If you have found this book useful you may be interested in other titles from Gower

Design Against Crime
Caroline L. Davey, Andrew B. Wootton and Mike P. Press
978-0-7546-4501-6

Design for Inclusivity
Roger Coleman, John Clarkson, Hua Dong and Julia Cassim
978-0-566-08707-3

Design for Healthcare
Chris Rust
978-0-7546-4530-6

Design for Micro-Utopias
John Wood
978-0-7546-4608-2

Design for Sustainability
Tracy Bhamra and Vicky Lofthouse
978-0-566-08704-2

How to Market Design Consultancy Services
Shan Preddy
978-0-566-08594-9

The Design Experience
Mike Press and Rachel Cooper
978-0-566-07891-0

Design Project Management
Griff Boyle
978-0-7546-1831-7

For further information on these and all our titles visit our website – www.gowerpub.com
All online orders receive a discount

GOWER